Cash Cow Casa: 51 Ways to Make Your

Note to Readers:
This publication is designed to provide accurate and authoritative information in regard to the subject matter covered. It is based upon sources believed to be accurate and reliable and is intended to be current as of the time it was written. It is sold with the understanding that neither the author nor the publisher is engaged in rendering legal, accounting, or other professional services. If legal advice or other expert assistance is required, the services of a competent professional person should be sought. Also, to confirm that the information has not been affected or changed by recent developments, traditional legal research techniques should be used, including checking primary sources where appropriate.

Based on the Declaration of Principles jointly adopted by a Committee of the American Bar Association and a Committee of Publishers and Associations.

Table of Contents

Chapter One. You don't have to move!

If you're a homeowner at risk of foreclosure, hopefully this book will put a smile back on your face, some serious jingle in your pocket, and a strategy in place for staying afloat in tough times. Not sure you're at risk? Here are the top three warning signs:

- You used to think nobody cared when your phone rarely rang. Then you missed a couple of house payments.
- You're glad gas prices have fallen so you can afford it if you have to move into your car.
- You're ready to say, "Let's make a deal" and trade your upside-down house for whatever's behind Door #3.

Seriously, here's the good news: Your home represents a significant asset that can bring you money in ways you may never have considered. This book gives you the inside story on how to put your house to work and earn its keep while you're busy earning a living holding down a job. Turning your home into a *cash cow casa* allows you to add additional streams of income that could keep you afloat in tough times or add to your coffers for the future.

This book…
…Is NOT about home-based businesses where YOU have to do most of the work… although dozens of these tips could lead to an exciting new business idea for you.
…Is NOT about how to save money or spend less on your home… although these strategies do provide viable options to survive tough times.
…Is NOT about borrowing money on your home or treating it as a virtual ATM (as many of us did in past years) except for several "special case" loans available only to special groups in certain geographic areas.

This book…
…Does give you dozens of specific ideas and examples of how homeowners are receiving up to six-figure incomes each year from alternative uses of their homes.
…Details dozens of tried-and-true moneymaking schemes and coordinates with additional information and resources on the associated website at *CashCowCasa.com*.
…Helps you see your property in brand new ways and visualize possibilities for revenue that may not have occurred to you. For

example, that roof over your head doesn't just keep the rain out; it could be the site of a lucrative cell tower rental or a solar energy system that brings in thousands of dollars annually.

…<u>Gives you insider information</u> about what other homeowners are doing along with the pitfalls you'll want to avoid. You'll find out exactly how much other homeowners are receiving for each of the cash cow strategies. For example, learn the inside details of payments to host a music video in the backyard or have a commercial filmed in the kitchen.

Only a few short years ago, you could milk cash out of your home by *borrowing* more against it--taking out a second or third mortgage. It was common practice to treat one's home as a virtual ATM machine and pull out cash through successive refinances as appraised values rose over time.

The days of rampant appreciation have disappeared along with the ability to rely on your house as an instant source of funds—*borrowed* funds, that is. Since most homes have declined dramatically in value in the last few years, the option to borrow more money against a home's value is largely off the table for most homeowners.

Today many homeowners can't sell and move if they wanted to, because there is not sufficient equity to pay off the existing mortgages. Nearly one-third of homeowners with a mortgage are underwater according to Zillow.[1] On average, U.S. homeowners owe about $75,000 more than what their house is worth.[2] Many homeowners opt to rent out their home and move to something less expensive to make ends meet. That approach is more risky than you might imagine, which is why it's considered the last resort and covered at the end of this book as strategy #51.

Nowadays it takes ingenuity and some effort to coax cash from your home. The good news is that many homeowners are doing just that and so can you! There are literally dozens of tried-and-true ways to generate cash flow from your property while you're busy doing other things like trying to keep your job.

If you are facing tough times and possibly even foreclosure, just one or two workable ideas in these pages could help you keep your home and stay afloat until the economy improves.

Unlock Cash By Thinking Outside the Box

Did you ever play the "101 Uses of a Wire Coat Hanger" game? The #1 purpose is to hang coats or clothes and then the fun starts as you come up with alternative uses: drain cleaner, car door opener, big bubble blower, emergency car radio aerial, stick for roasting marshmallows, frame for a dream-catcher or kite, etc. You get the idea.

The key to turning your home into a *cash cow casa* is to apply the "101 Uses" game to your property and try to see it in an entirely new light. Every part of your residence already has its standard, defined purpose. To unlock your home's hidden cash potential, you'll need to think outside the box and "re-purpose" your property with cash flow in mind.

Here are a few ways you can re-think and re-purpose your home into a *cash cow casa*:

- The obvious purpose of your garage is to park your cars (although 75% of garages are too stuffed with Stuff to house a car[3]), but a garage can be re-purposed for a variety of income-producing uses: a storage unit, a warehouse and order processing facility, a rehearsal studio. The list is limited only by your ability to brainstorm the possibilities.
- Your yard provides opportunities for recreation or enjoyment of nature, but a yard can be re-purposed as a wedding venue, film location, place for outdoor advertising, special event locale, plot for a cash crop, and so much more.
- The main purpose of owning your property is to have a primary residence, but your title to the property can generate cash if you share equity with a partner, sell certain rights, qualify for a government subsidy or tax credit, or collect referral fees.

The examples presented in this volume represent only a starting point of what's possible and what other homeowners have done. In order to make these methods work for you, you'll have to adjust them to your own situation.

Scale Up, Scale Down, Adapt These Strategies

For each of the tips in this book, you'll need to make adjustments based on your own home, community, and circumstances. Since most of the examples in these pages come from homes in relatively "upscale" areas, the examples cited here may need to be scaled down for your particular locale.

Homes of all sizes have the potential to become *cash cow casas*. The average size of a new home in the U.S. is now about 2,400 square feet[4], down considerably from recent years but far larger than the 1970 average of 1,400 square feet. The trend to smaller homes will continue into 2015 according to building professionals[5]. Size matters for many of the strategies presented here. If you are living in a home that is significantly smaller than the average home, you still can benefit from this book, but you may have to adapt the ideas and scale down your expectations.

Once you've read the book, I challenge you to tailor these ideas to your own situation or to invent an entirely new way to have your house generate cash flow! Please share your ideas and experience with others on our website at *CashCowCasa.com*.

The "Inconvenience" of Living in a *Cash Cow Casa*

Most of the possibilities presented here entail a certain amount of inconvenience or loss of privacy. If you are independently wealthy, you might want to put this book back on the shelf right now since you surely wouldn't want to be inconvenienced by having other people use parts of your property.

However, if you face the prospect of moving from your comfortable 3- or 4-bedroom home with a garage and nice yard to a 1- or 2-bedroom apartment with a common parking area and no yard, you might be willing to endure a little inconvenience!

Here's what's truly inconvenient:
- Packing up all of your belongings and having to move.
- Squeezing your family into a smaller space with fewer beds and baths.
- Getting rid of belongings so your Stuff will fit into a downsized home.
- Giving up your attached 2- or 3-car garage for a common parking lot many steps from your front door.
- Foregoing your private laundry room for a communal laundry facility or commercial laundromat.
- Trading your private backyard for a crowded common area on the grounds of an apartment building.

You see the point. Some of the opportunities outlined in this book require a greater degree of inconvenience or effort on your part to accomplish. However, the drawbacks of pursuing a *cash cow casa* strategy pale in comparison to the downright annoying alternatives!

Sometimes the inconveniences turn out to be opportunities in disguise. At first, I found location rentals very inconvenient. Now I don't mind when my kitchen is rented out for a film shoot. I snack less, save some calories, and enjoy rubbing elbows with the crew during the catered group meals. When film shoots go overtime—

and so many do—I know I'll be pocketing extra cash as the contract calls for a time-and-a-half rental fee.

You'll find "Do's and Don'ts" for each of the first several dozen strategies in this book. The guidelines will help you minimize the inconvenience or hassle of living in a *cash cow casa*.

How Much Time Will Your *Cash Cow Casa* Require?

The strategies presented in this book will require some level of effort on your part to accomplish although the assumption is that you will keep your day job while your *house* goes to work for *you*. In many cases, your involvement will be no more than simply finding an *agent* and interacting with that person who will take care of most of the details for you.

However, some of the activities described in these pages will require your time and effort to accomplish. If the anticipated payoff does not justify the investment of your own time and attention, consider involving your children. Many of these ideas make ideal projects for older children or teenagers. Kids love to be helpful, especially if their efforts result in a share of the profits.

Finally, check the companion website at *CashCowCasa.com* for help and support. You'll find *FastStart* options there to get the ball rolling as well as important contacts, local agents, and other helpful information.

Disclaimers, Restrictions, and Limitations

You'll need to check local ordinances and zoning restrictions in your area as well as any homeowner association rules that may block or restrict implementation of some of these strategies for your property. Although you may not be able to implement a particular idea exactly as presented, the basic concept might be adaptable to fit the limitations of your situation.

Perhaps the most challenging restrictions come from homeowner associations of gated communities. Many of the practices presented here involve traffic to your home. The question is: Will those vehicles be allowed through the gate? A relatively small TV commercial, for example, typically would include several large trucks of lighting and camera equipment along with a dozen cars for the crew and cast members. If the vehicles do succeed in coming through the gate, will the association object to so many vehicles parked on the street near your home? You'll need to check the fine print of your association rules.

You might still be able to make money from location rentals if you live in a gated community governed by a homeowner association, but you may have to scale down to a smaller production such as a *webisode* video or still photography shoot. Equipment for small productions could fit in a van rather than in those large box trucks used for standard productions. Crewmembers can park outside and carpool through the gate so only a couple vehicles would be showing up at your home. Better yet, offer the homeowner's association a cut of the profits.

County or city zoning rules may preclude your ability to implement some of these strategies. Find the zoning department website for your area and type in your address to see the zoning category of your property. The government website will probably have an explanation of the various zoning categories so you can discover what you can and cannot do on your property.

Finally, you may want to consult with an attorney or financial professional for their assistance in implementing some of these strategies. If legal or financial advice or other expert assistance is required, the services of a competent professional should be sought.

Chapter Two. Location Rentals & Events

Tapping into the lucrative entertainment field is a great way to generate large sums of cash from your home. You don't have to own a fancy mansion close to Hollywood studios to get in on the bonanza of film location rentals—although that wouldn't hurt. Properties of all styles and sizes across the U.S. and in other countries garner big bucks to host feature films, made-for-TV movies, commercials, reality TV shows, photo shoots and more.

Many producers are looking for a "typical home" to use for their project. Sometimes an average looking home can be the hardest type for a producer to find since so few owners register a standard home with a film location agency. So don't skip this chapter based on an erroneous assumption that your house has to be unique, photogenic, or large.

Let's start with a little game of *Jeopardy*. Knowing that the answer is an empathic *No!*, what is the correct question?
A. *"As your long-time friend, can my band use your living room to shoot a demo video for the web? I promise, you'll hardly know we're there."*
B. *"Can we rent your house for my upcoming feature film that I wrote and will produce myself? We don't have a budget right now but can pay you on the backend."*
C. *"Can we use your grassy yard later today and tomorrow to shoot some stunts? We don't have time to get a film permit but don't worry because we'll have a medic there."*
D. All of the above

If you answered *D*, good for you, continue reading this section. If not (Really?), hopefully reading this chapter will temper your trusting soul a bit when it comes to the reality of productions. Focus especially on the "Don'ts" that will alert you to the potential downside of this upbeat business.

Many films and television shows are produced in a studio environment, but production companies often want to shoot all or a portion of the project "on location." Production companies need locations for feature films, television programs, commercials and other shoots. Location rental agencies meet this need by serving as the matchmakers between production companies and you, the owner of a prospective location.

Exodus of Productions from Hollywood

Hollywood has been the undisputed "entertainment capital of the world," and location rentals have been prevalent near Hollywood. During the last decade, however, the trend has been for production to move out of California to other states and countries.

Now only 10 percent of the new hour-long network dramas this season are being produced in Southern California, down from 50 percent in 2010 and down from nearly 80 percent in 2005.[6] TV productions are moving elsewhere to save costs and enjoy more favorable tax treatment than they receive in California. Producers are finding more production-friendly venues in New York, North Carolina, Georgia and other states.

The impact of the exodus is far reaching as the wealth generated by television production is spread around the country if not the world. According to the Los Angeles County Economic Development group, a typical network series has a budget of $60 million and generates 840 jobs, either directly or indirectly.

The stats bring unwelcome news to *cash cow casa* owners near Hollywood, but the spread of wealth means that location rentals could occur virtually anywhere. In addition, considering the rise of webisodes, web ads, and local productions, you could snag a location rental regardless of where you're located.

1. Garner thousands per day to host commercials.

You don't have to own a large, fancy home to attract commercials. Many homes have at least one special feature or focal point that could be featured in a commercial. Think about each area of your home inside and out and try to envision what area would work as a location for a commercial.

Knowing Your Home's Strengths

One weekend at a friend's house, I noticed their lovely kitchen situated in a large rectangular area also containing the dining and family areas. The house is a typical-sized home that is not photogenic except for the kitchen. I used my cell phone to take several pictures of the pretty kitchen making sure to show the wide-open spaces on two sides of it, which would accommodate lighting and camera equipment. I emailed the photos and description to several location rental agencies. One agency responded favorably and immediately sent a scout to the house.

In order to host a commercial, you'll need ample parking space nearby and somewhere to place the portable power generator that the production company brings. If it won't fit on the driveway, they may be able to place it on the street in front of the house.

Commercials often have a short turnaround time. Final decisions about using your location may not be made until the last minute since the ad executives may fly in from out of town; they'll want to see the various prospective locations before selecting the one to use. You need to remain flexible and remember that nothing is certain until you receive a signed contract AND the check.

Getting Star Struck

Unless you serve as your own site rep, homeowners typically are not welcome on the set. Luckily, I have met quite a few of the famous folks who have come to our *cash cow casa* and can tell you, for what it's worth, that most of them have been friendly and look just as good in person as they do on screen.

It's actually quite fascinating if you do have the opportunity to chat with these famous folks. Not too long ago, I had the chance to eat dinner at the table with a young lady we've all heard of. She shared many stories. But there was one story that I still wonder about.

The star was recounting her discovery and the early days of her stardom when she still had to hold down a "day job." After getting laid off from that job, she received unemployment compensation. Then BEFORE she got her first big (and I mean BIG) check from one of the top entertainment companies, she claimed that she looked at her unemployment check—I believe she said it was $900—and "TORE IT UP" because she felt she was worth so much more than that! I gasped audibly and we all laughed. Hey, I think I'm worth more than my year's salary, but I don't think I'll be tearing that up anytime soon.

We once hosted a commercial featuring a famous athlete who played the role of a new resident setting up TV/internet service upon moving into his new home. We never saw him. They whisked him in and out of the property so fast that we didn't even catch a glimpse.

From Zero to Hollywood in One Day

The shoot involving the famous athlete took a total of three days: one day to prep several rooms in our home by stacking (empty) moving boxes and arranging furnishings and equipment for the shoot, a full day of shooting for the 30-second commercial, and a strike day to put everything back as it was. Happily, the commercial brought us five figures!

The production crew needed only a couple rooms in our home, but you can't imagine the maze of wires, crowd of people, multitude of vehicles, and abundance of production equipment required to shoot that commercial, considered rather modest by industry standards.

A modest commercial may entail 25 to 35 or more people coming to your property. Do you have adequate street parking? Besides the passenger vehicles, there will be several large production trucks to carry lighting and camera equipment.

If you're lucky enough to snag a commercial, your quiet and peaceful abode will burst into a noisy beehive of activity for a few days. You may be asked to move out since expensive and sensitive equipment will be set up and left overnight when the crew goes home after each 12- to 14-hour day. If you do stay elsewhere, the producer may hire an around-the-clock security detail to keep an eye on the property. Some of those high-end cameras are worth over a million dollars!

Commercials pay *what*?

You can tolerate hassles and scheduling pressures when you discover how lucrative commercials can be. Homeowners receive up to **$2,500 to $5,000 per day** or more. You collect the most money for a day that entails actual filming and half of the shooting-day fee for days spent preparing the set or restoring your property to its original condition, referred to as "prep" and "strike" days, respectively.

If production requires extensive use of your home inside and out or if they make major modifications to your home, you should expect a higher fee. Sometimes the producer will want to paint or add a facade for a special look. You'll automatically be paid more (i.e. for more "strike" days) since it takes time to re-paint back to the original colors after the shoot.

Top Do's and Don'ts for Hosting Commercials

- Do insist on having a site rep: the person who keeps an eye on things and looks out for your property. During one commercial shoot, a site rep I know heard a loud snap and noticed two crewmembers standing on the breakfast counter in order to change some hanging light fixtures when the granite cracked under their weight. After the production ended, a specialist glued and repainted the crack so skillfully that most homeowners would not have noticed the damage unless they scrutinized the counter for it specifically. Luckily, the site rep had witnessed the break and reported it to the homeowners who had to file an insurance claim.

- <u>Do</u> require the production company to install layout board to protect your floors. It's like lining your floors with smooth cardboard. Camera and lighting equipment can scratch your floors and you simply won't believe the number of people it takes to shoot a 30-second commercial who will be walking on your floors so you'll want them protected.
- <u>Do</u> expect production to bring a large, stand-alone power generator to provide power. Commercials require enormous amounts of electricity, and you don't want production to tie into your house power. If they do use the house power, it could cost you hundreds of dollars and risk damage to existing circuits not designed for intensive power use.

- <u>Don't</u> forget to check the functioning of appliances after the shoot. One time we moved back in after a 4-day commercial shoot and got sick from eating food that had been in the frig. We later learned that a blown circuit cut power to the refrigerator for three days and most of the food had spoiled. The production company failed to mention the problem initially but later did own up to the problem and reimbursed us for the cost of replacing the spoiled food.
- <u>Don't</u> shoot a commercial without proper third party insurance and a security deposit. As mentioned earlier, one homeowner's granite countertop cracked under the weight of two lighting specialists who stood on the unsupported, protruding breakfast counter to change light fixtures above. The security deposit might have been sufficient to cover the cost of replacing just the breakfast counter itself. However, to prevent mismatched counters throughout the kitchen, all of the granite needed replacement at the same time, which necessitated a claim on the producer's insurance that named the homeowner as the insured third party.
- <u>Don't</u> expect to meet the talent. The actors in a commercial—especially if they are "big names"—are whisked in and out so fast that you barely see them.

2. Get top money for TV programs or feature films.

This type of location rental is the most intensive and requires a property with sufficient space inside and out to accommodate a large crew with lots of equipment. You'll need to have ample parking space on or near your property. For feature films, you'll need a very large and accessible area nearby that can accommodate equipment trucks and star wagons the size of semi-trailer trucks.

Here's where you get a true taste of Hollywood, literally! Everyone on the set has a specialized job including the professional cooks who prepare fresh meals on site to feed the crew. Starting early in the morning, a breakfast cook makes fresh omelets to order.

Then a lunch cook takes over followed later by a cook for supper/dinner. The crew often welcomes homeowners to join the feast since there are plenty of P.A.'s (production assistants) and other people to look out for you on the set.

Welcome to Hollywood!
Shoots in this category may be done for a television mini-series, a made-for-television movie, an episodic TV show, or scenes in a feature film. In any case, you can expect the cast and crew to number nearly 50 to 100 or more people.

Within hours after the first truck arrives, your property will be transformed from a quiet residence to a bustling flurry of activity with people rushing every which way, seemingly thousands of miles of cables running in and out of your home, noisy trucks rumbling outside, tents around your home to house equipment or food service, crew coming in and out, lots of people talking to one another over walkie-talkies and more commotion that you ever thought possible on your property!

There are plenty of fun moments and photo ops for the homeowner. During one film shoot at our *cash cow casa*, I snapped a digital photo of two gorgeous bright red, high-end sports cars sitting in our garage. The producer told me that they were worth a million bucks each! I printed the snapshot and put it in our family photo album for posterity. I can picture our descendants someday flipping through our photo albums and wondering how we fell from those million-dollar rides into the humble vehicles of subsequent photos.

The Issue of Extras
One thing to be wary of during a larger production is the presence of "extras" on the set. As a general rule, TV and film shoots are surprisingly professional in that every person knows his or her role in the project and executes it with great professionalism. Extras, however, do not fit this rule. They generally are not union members, not experts in any technical field (lighting, camera, sound etc.), nor are they talented actors. They are extra bodies needed to fill in a particular scene such as a crowd scene. When they're not participating in that scene, they have nothing to do and could end up causing trouble.

I once found extras intruding into an unused room in our home looking in drawers and closets. "Well EXCUUUUSE ME!" I belted out in fine Steve Martin fashion. They probably were just being nosey so we laughed it off and let it go. But after that encounter I did go lock all the doors to unused areas and kept an eye out for stray extras wandering around.

It's a good idea to ask ahead of time about the presence of extras and how they will be managed. The production company should have some type of security present if more than a few extras will be coming to your house. At the very minimum, there should be a site rep that keeps tabs on the extras. The issue of extras ought to be spelled out in the contract prior to the start of production.

Luckily, You Don't Always Get What You Want

Homeowners aspire to get lucrative TV and film shoots, but you don't get every project that's scouted and sometimes that's a blessing. Well, initially it's very disappointing when your house is scouted, seriously considered, but then passed over in favor of the competition.

One time our home was scouted but not selected as the location for an opening scene in a movie. I was disappointed until hearing what the scene depicted: An enraged husband drives up to the front door of the house, storms up the staircase to the master bathroom and murders his wife who's bathing in the tub, then flees back down the stairs and speeds off after the crime is committed. Whew! Make-believe or not, I'm sure glad that didn't happen at my house!

TV and Film Shoots pay *what?*

Major projects for film and TV pay the highest location fees. As with commercials and other types of shoots, you receive the most money for a day that entails actual filming and half as much for prep and strike days. Shoots for TV and film scenes may last from three to five days. Remember, in this industry, a "day" refers to a 12-hour or even a 14-hour day.

Homeowners are receiving up to **$5,000 to $7,500 per day** or more for larger projects. I know homeowners who receive more for homes that are high end and well located. These shoots are the most desirable and lucrative in the industry from the homeowner's point of view, but are increasingly harder to get during these challenging economic times.

Like every industry in recent years, production companies are seeking less expensive alternatives and are finding them in "webisodes," which are productions published on the Internet. Increasingly, producers need locations for shooting webisodes. As you might guess, those shoots don't pay as well. You would be lucky to receive up to **$1,000 to $1,500** per day. Hey, most of us would be delighted with that amount, right?

If you want to get started as a location for filming and you are located within an hour's drive of a film school, you might consider calling the school to offer your home as a potential filming location for student projects. They don't pay well if at all—perhaps several hundred dollars per day—but it's a great way to jump into the industry and learn right along with the student producers. You just might make some valuable contacts that will pay off down the line.

Top Do's and Don'ts for TV and Film Shoots

- <u>Do</u> go over the contract with a fine-tooth comb and don't hesitate to ask for changes and additions. A no-smoking policy inside the home should be stated right in the contract. Another provision should be a requirement to install layout board before bringing in equipment. Rely on an experienced location rental agent or consult with a knowledgeable attorney as you negotiate the contract with the production company.
- <u>Do</u> expect some Hollywood magic. Your grass may be sprayed green, a grove of trees may appear magically, or the color of your house may change. No matter. They'll put it all back as it was when they're finished. You might get a free paint job out of it like we did.
- Do a very thorough Final Walkthrough at the end of the rental to assess damages inside and out. Test the functioning of everything. If you have a sprinkler system in your yard, you better check to make sure that the system functions properly by putting it through its paces. If crewmembers pulled heavy carts of equipment over the lawn, it's likely that they broke a few sprinkler heads or worse. We learned this one the hard way.

- <u>Don't</u> allow any personal use of the premises during a rental. I came home during a film rental one hot summer day—that was not supposed to include use of the pool—to find that crew members had invited friends over for a swim in the pool. Talk about liability! Using the pool without permission also means using it without the proper cleaning, preparation, and safety measures.
- <u>Don't</u> permit children on the set. This rule also applies to all other types of location rentals. The crews' friends mentioned above also brought their children who ran on the deck and jumped into the pool as I walked into the backyard. What a scary sight! Luckily, no child got hurt that day. The presence of children on a production set is fraught with danger due to the fact that the production typically fills the property with miles of cables, banks of electrical outlets, expensive cameras, delicate and often hot lighting equipment, and many busy

adults rushing this way and that who are too distracted with the shoot to watch out for a child's well-being. Ditto for crewmembers' pets. A production location is absolutely no place for children or pets.

- Don't forget the "wear and tear" factor when figuring your earnings. Production companies will pay you for damaging your home during a shoot, but you receive no compensation for "normal" wear and tear based on their expected use. The intense use given by 50 crewmembers over 20 days, equates to 1,000 days, or about 3 years, of wear and tear. You'll notice the walls need a fresh coat of paint and the floors need refinishing. Blinds and shades need cleaning and repairing. Your furnace ductwork needs cleaning and filters need changing. Windows and screens may need adjustment or repair. All those things add up and should be figured into the CDB—the cost of doing business.

3. Collect big bucks to have a music video.

Have you heard the secret of how a musician can end up with $1,000,000 as a performer? The answer: start out with two million dollars! Except for the top stars, most musicians operate on a very tight budget. Music videos don't pay as well as commercials but chances are you'll enjoy hosting music videos more if you've done the proper planning and have a solid contract.

Preparing for an Entourage
From the homeowner's perspective, a successful music video is all about managing the entourage, which can be sizeable for a full-fledged music video. (Remember, you can scale the numbers down if it's a "mini" music video, but the same general principles apply.)

You'll need ample space and proper planning to accommodate the inevitable throng of people—expect at least 50 or more followers—who attend the music video: the musicians' family members, friends, business associates, those associates' friends…the list goes on. Is it likely to be a hot day or a rainy day? The entourage will need adequate cover. What about food and snacks? Bathroom facilities? Disposal of trash? Crowd management and security? Parking? All of these matters need to be handled by the producers as specified in the contract and not left up to chance or to the homeowner.

Think of a music video as part "video production" and part "large party." The latter aspect of music videos requires a number of special measures not typical for other location rental projects. All of those special measures should be spelled out in the contract:

- The number of guests allowed as part of the entourage and the designated area where they will stay;

- Provisions for feeding, seating, and handling the guests;
- Areas where smoking is allowed with appropriate receptacles for cigarette butts;
- The number of security guards to be hired and their duties and assignments; and
- Arrangements for clean-up and trash removal.

The Inside Story of Music Videos

Some years ago we hosted our first music video and it was a learning experience. For one thing, I learned that even artists your kids have heard of probably have severely limited budgets when it comes to shooting their music video. They may have spared no expense producing their CD in the music studio to get the right sound but now need to share the video venue—and split the costs—with another artist or two for the day. Guess what! That means you've got several entourages to deal with, as if one weren't enough!

Luckily our agent had plenty of experience with music videos and insisted that the producer arrange for three or four people to work security. It seemed like overkill until the day of the music video arrived along with more people than had ever been on our property! Without security making sure that the entourage stayed in their designated area outside, our home would have been overrun.

More recently, our son got to participate in a music video shot at our *cash cow casa*. The producers needed extras to appear in a dance scene as the artists sang (well, lip-synched actually). So he got to have some fun and get in on the action. In my blog the next day, I remarked about when the teenager is happy, the entire family is happy. Who knew that a *cash cow casa* could bring so much fun and joy!

Music Videos pay *what*?

Going rates of location rentals for music videos vary widely depending on the popularity of the musical group. Generally, the rate will be less than for TV programs and commercials but more than for reality TV shows and still shoots.

Based on my own experience and that of other homeowners I've interviewed, the rates for music video location rentals range from up to **$2,000 to $3,500 for the day** or more if your home is exceptionally large or offers a special view or other special feature. I recently spoke with the owner of a lovely home on the beach with plenty of parking along the street, and he told me he receives between $7,500 and $10,000 per day since the video can be shot in the house, yard, and also on the wide sandy beach! He actually used the term *cash cow* to describe his house during our conversation.

If the shoot extends an hour or two past the contracted duration (which is normally a 12- to 14-hour day), then an overtime fee kicks in. Generally, overtime pays you time-and-a-half per hour for every hour or 15-minute portion thereof.

Music videos are notorious for going overtime. It could be the confusion that often occurs when you have so many people on set. Or perhaps it's the fact that many musicians are more comfortable in the late evening hours. In any case, you can anticipate that a music video just might go overtime.

Top Do's and Don'ts for Music Videos

- Do restrict the size of the musician's entourage or you could have hundreds of people show up. Stipulate the restriction in writing as part of the contract. If there are several artists there simultaneously, decide ahead of time how you will limit more than one entourage.
- Do insist that the producers arrange for adequate security. They'll need at least three security guards, possibly more. One guard keeps the bulk of the entourage out of the house; another is assigned to keep the entourage quiet and well behaved. And the third guard should be stationed out front or at the driveway to prevent uninvited guests from coming onto the property. For this type of rental, it helps if your property is fully fenced so access can be restricted to one area for ingress and egress.
- Do add a non-smoking clause to the contract. Besides the smoky smell and butts left behind, it's dangerous to have smokers milling around inside or outside your home with all the hot lighting equipment and other distractions.

- Don't leave your property during a music video; it's better for a family member to stay on site and help the security guards and site rep keep an eye on the place. In case your family does need to leave the property during the shoot, move your cars out of the garage and park them on the street prior to the start of the shoot for easy egress if needed.
- Don't rush into contract negotiations for a music video or grant a request for a "friend's" band to shoot their latest video at your house. Music videos require careful planning and extra contract provisions necessitated by the addition of an entourage to the normal numbers of cast and crew. You'll need to agree on the arrangements and payments for food, seating, security, portable toilets, exterior and interior cleanup, trash removal etc.

- <u>Don't</u> allow guests to wander around your property. Security should make sure that the entourage stays in the assigned area. Smoking should be confined to an outside smoking area with proper receptacles available.

4. *Book a reality television show for gobs of cash.*

Your home might be suitable for this type of rental if it has at least three or four bedrooms and if your family is willing to relocate during the rental. Although it helps to have a large home for reality shoots, you don't need as much parking to host a reality show as you would need for other types of film location rentals. Reality show participants don't bring cars, and fewer crewmembers are needed than for the other types of productions.

As I write this, my family and I await the start of a reality television show that will take place in our home over the course of about eight weeks. It will be a complete "takeover" during which time we must relocate to a hotel or other facility at the producer's expense. Yes, it's an inconvenience but one we're happy to endure given that the production company pays us more than many folks make in a year—and it's all paid upfront before we move out!

The Reality Behind Reality Shows

The best thing about location rentals is that the homeowner receives every penny of the rental fee upfront! That's a major advantage to standard residential rentals where you rent out your home long-term to a private party and then hope and pray every month that the tenant will pay the rent. (All too often, they don't.)

The biggest negative of a reality show rental is that production does a complete "takeover" of your property and you have to move out. Happily, you generally receive a relocation fee that covers the cost of staying in an extended stay hotel during the shoot. Realize, however, that most of those places are 2 or, at most, 3 bedroom suites so it can be tight quarters if your family is large or used to more space.

The producer also pays to move or store your belongings during the rental. The production company hires a professional mover and pays the full cost to pack your belongings, move everything into storage (or another home if you prefer), and then put it all back at the end of the rental.

The movers take pictures of everything for reference so that they can restore your home to its original arrangement, but believe me, perfect restoration never happens. It all works out well enough if you don't mind that the lamp got moved over there, you find a rug or plant in the wrong room, and the contents of your bookshelves are rearranged.

Both the rental fee and the relocation fee are paid in full upfront before you move out but not so for the utilities and any L&D (loss and damage) settlements. It's important that the agent collect a security deposit that is sufficient to cover the projected amount for these items. And remember that you can't estimate utilities based on what your family typically uses since there will be far more people using the utilities. We've found that our electric bill is more than 10 times higher than "normal" when our *cash cow casa* hosts a large reality show during the summer months. My family hardly uses air conditioning when we're at home, but the AC is cranked to the max 24/7 during a location rental.

You can imagine how quickly the costs add up if your utility bills are many times greater than normal. It's wise to have the production company pay the utility bills as they come due and not wait to the end of the production to settle up. Then as long as the agent has collected a suitable security deposit, the ending utility charges and any damages should be covered.

The Good, The Bad, and The Ugly

The fun really starts after the show is done and you can tell your friends to watch your home on TV. We've had calls and emails from friends and relatives around the country as they see our home in a starring role.

Not everyone in the family raves about the shows we've done. One reality show that aired on a major network re-purposed our son's large bedroom into a lounge for couples to meet during a dating reality show. As a young teen at the time, all he could say was, "Yuck!!!" at the fact that people had been hugging and kissing in his bedroom.

One of the most exciting experiences for me occurred during a reality show about Russian opera singers coming to Hollywood to be discovered. (The show was only aired outside of the U. S.) The evening that the singing contestants arrived was absolutely magical as our home quickly filled with the sounds and energy of young men excited about coming to Southern California and Hollywood.

Several young opera singers gathered around the piano to sing "O Solo Mio" in Italian. It's one thing to hear opera on stage (or film); it's quite another to hear opera singers in your own living room, belting out a favorite song loud enough to vibrate the windows! It certainly was an evening to remember. And I felt like we did our little part to improve international relations a bit.

Then we had the reality show about people trying to overcome a mental/personality disorder that seemed to go very well during production. However, as we later watched the show, we discovered that one guy acted so weird and threatening that he was asked to leave and another guy contemplated attacking the other contestants with a knife! Visions of lawsuits and liability immediately came to mind as we watched. Luckily it all worked out fine, but it made us realize that location rentals could turn out badly.

Perhaps the biggest shock, however, came as we watched yet another dating reality series that had been filmed at our *cash cow casa* over the course of several months. Much to our chagrin, several men had taken their clothes off and paraded around the house in the nude as cameras continued rolling. Thankfully before the show aired, the producers positioned the show's logo strategically, fig-leaf-fashioned, so that no nudity appeared on the screen. Frankly, I was embarrassed by the incident and surprised that a major network would air the scene even with the superimposed "fig leafs."

Lesson learned: Besides having proper liability insurance in place, hire a very meticulous, world-class cleaning crew to do the most thorough house-cleaning job after a reality show since you just never know what went on while you were away!

Reality TV pays *what*?
This type of location rental pays less than some of the other types of shoots on a per-day basis but the property is rented for many days so the total payment adds up to a large sum. A typical reality show rental could last 4 to 6 weeks or up to 3 months! Homeowners receive up to **$800 to $1,200 per day** or even more if your home is large, spectacular, or in a special location such as on the beach or overlooking a panoramic view.

One of the things happening with greater frequency lately is that producers are trolling the real estate multiple listing services for potential locations. The problem is that many real estate agents have little if any experience with the location rental business. Signing a standard lease with a location rental company is fraught with problems and risks not encountered in standard residential rentals. It's better for you as a homeowner to deal with a specialized location rental agent who understands this business.

Top Do's and Don'ts for Reality TV

- <u>Do</u> require the producer to pay all utilities during their stay since your utility bills could be 5 to 10 times higher than normal. Collect a sufficient security deposit to more than cover the estimated utility bills and likely potential damages.
- <u>Do</u> record and take photos of utility meters both upon move-in and move-out so the charges can be prorated. You or your agent can find helpful instructions at each utility's website about how to read meters and calculate usage. When prorating, charge production's usage rate at the highest tier if your utility rates are tiered. Your location rental agent really should take care of this task for you, but many of them don't. They'll do a fast proration that probably would not be favorable to you.
- <u>Do</u> insist on high-quality professional movers who take photos of everything, including every shelf and cabinet, before they pack and move your belongings. They'll use those photos as reference for putting everything back as it was or, at least, similar to how it was.

- <u>Don't</u> move out 100 percent of your belongings for a reality show. The producers do not need every inch of space; they just don't want your personal belongings to disappear or be damaged since they'd have to pay for any loss or damage. Have a locksmith install those small round locks on many of your cabinet doors and drawers. Keep a locked 4-drawer file of important papers or personal items in a locked closet. Add locks to your garage storage cabinets. If you need a particular paper or item during the rental, the producer generally will allow you access long enough to retrieve it.
- <u>Don't</u> rush the final walkthrough or try to handle it on your own. Bring help! Was heavy equipment rolled through the yard? If so, have someone check for damage to plants and sprinklers. Did they place lights on the roof? If so, get a roofer to inspect for damage. And despite your very best efforts, expect that you will discover hidden damage later on after the production company is long gone.
- <u>Don't</u> rely solely on your agent to handle all negotiations especially at the end of a shoot regarding loss and damages. You know your property better than the agent. If you see extra tire marks on the driveway or scuffs on the floor, insist on cleaning and restoration. Obtain several written estimates from qualified contractors. It will be worth your time and effort in persuading the producer to compensate you fairly for any damages.

5. Get paid handsomely for still photo shoots.

Photographers need a variety of settings for shooting products and people for advertisements in magazines and other print media. You don't have to have a large or fancy home to get still photo shoots. You may be able to take advantage of this source of cash even if you live in a gated community since there are only a few vehicles that need to come to your house.

Don't Assume What Look They Want

We once had a rental of our pool to shoot a magazine ad for a national face cream product. They selected us because our salt-water pool would be easy on the eyes of their underwater models. The models, with flawless skin, stayed underwater for long periods of time with open eyes, smiling at the camera. A typical chlorinated pool would have caused red, stinging eyes in short order.

It seemed ironic that our pool was selected since it's a simple rectangular pool with a blue fiberglass surface, a regular "Plain Jane" pool. You'd think that an advertiser would want an upscale pool with curvy shapes, waterfalls, decorative rock formations, or artistic mosaics. However, the producer wanted just what we had since it served as a clean, crisp underwater backdrop for their lovely models with clear skin.

Lesson learned: Homeowners can't make assumptions about what is "photogenic" and what look will appeal to a producer. Only the producer and other creative staff know what works for their particular project and purpose.

It's best if you (or a scout from a location rental agency) take profile pictures of your property from virtually every angle. The point is to provide the producers and creative team with a realistic view of your property inside and out.

You might not realize that your well-lighted staircase makes the perfect setting for a fashion shoot or that the birdbath next to your flowerbed provides an ideal showcase for outdoor home-and-garden products. The creative team, however, will see your property's potential for their projects and pay you cold, hard cash for the opportunity to realize their creative vision at your *cash cow casa*.

Still Shoots pay *what*?

This type of location rental pays the lowest amount on a per-day basis compared with other types of location rentals, but it's the easiest on you and your house. Photo shoots for national advertising campaigns pay well, almost as much as rental rates for hosting TV commercials. However, most of these shoots will pay far less than the standard rates that you would receive for a TV commercial.

Based on my own experience as well as that of other homeowners I've interviewed, rates range from up to **$1,500 to $2,500 a day** if the shoot is for a national ad campaign. Many still shoots, however, pay **less than $1000 per day**. These shoots may bring you up to **$500** or more for a session that lasts about five or six hours. Again, if you have a high-end home, you can expect more.

The great thing about still photo-shoots compared with video and film projects is that this type of rental puts less wear and tear on the house. There is far less equipment being dragged around than for other types of location rentals. For still photography, the crew brings hand-held cameras, tripods, and lighting equipment only. There is minimal setup and usually no need for layout board to protect the floors from the heavy equipment used during the other types of shoots.

Top Do's and Don'ts for Still Photo Shoots

- <u>Do</u> require a written contract with the responsible party and spell out all terms and conditions. Having a detailed contract protects you and should not be left out or glossed over simply because fewer people will be involved or because the shoot may be brief. Something to watch out for is when a photographer wants to "book" your house (without a contract or a flimsy contract) and then subcontracts to many other photographers to come shoot their models at your house. Hard telling what could happen and who would be responsible.
- <u>Do</u> find out how many people will be coming to the property. A photo shoot for a notable individual or group might entail an entourage in which case the contract should specify the limits and provisions for guests (see the section on Music Videos for further detail).
- <u>Do</u> ask your agent about the nature of the photo shoot and exactly what to expect especially if you have children. Be aware that models and actresses participating in a fashion shoot may change clothes as they hurry through a hallway in your home. Or the clothing to be photographed could be very skimpy.

- <u>Don't</u> allow a photo session without proper insurance naming you as a third party insured. Your homeowner's insurance doesn't go far enough to cover the types of perils inherent in any type of photo shoot or film location rental. The photographer or producer needs to have a temporary policy that covers property damage as well as liability.
- <u>Don't</u> let a still photo shoot turn into a video production since the latter constitutes a more intensive use of your property for which you should be compensated appropriately. Read the contract carefully; it should specifically state what type of photography is allowed.
- <u>Don't</u> worry that you could accidentally end up with inappropriate photography occurring on your property. The contract describes the

nature of the photography, and you can add a statement specifically prohibiting nudity and X-rated photography.

6. Host a wedding for a lucrative cut.

Do you have a pretty backyard with room for at least several large tables plus additional open space to spare? Wedding venues garner big bucks just to provide the location for the happy couple's special day. A few phone calls and research on the web will tell you what the main wedding venues are in your area and how much they charge. You may be surprised to discover the phenomenal sums people shell out for weddings these days despite the challenging economy!

Not every couple wants to wed in a busy hotel with other weddings going on at the same time. Your private location offers an alternative that gives the couple and their guests a level of attention, exclusivity, and privacy they cannot achieve at a hotel.

Many of the standard wedding venues insist on providing other services along with the location itself. For example, hotels often bundle the wedding venue with all other goods and services for the wedding: rental of tables, chairs, linens, china, flatware, glassware; all food and beverage service; floral and decorations; photography and so much more. These wedding packages come with hefty price tags so many couples look for *a la carte* alternatives and your location gives them the opportunity to arrange their own individual services.

Is Your Property Wedding-Bell Ready?

Your property will be ready to host a wedding once it achieves the 3 P's: *polished*, *pretty*, and *plenty of parking*. The yard and grounds should look well manicured with green grass and gleaming structures. You'll want to clean and *polish* your BBQ, pool, gazebo, walls or other surfaces.

The grounds should look *pretty* with blooming flowers, well-placed plants, and a few decorative items. You don't need much in the way of décor since wedding planners will bring their own decorations to fit the color scheme and theme of the wedding. The venue merely serves as a backdrop to the main look of the wedding.

Finally, there needs to be *parking* on or near your property. Could you arrange the use of a nearby vacant lot or street parking? As the provider of the location, you may or may not be expected to provide valet service for parking. Discuss with the wedding planner if they expect you to hire the parking attendants. If so, you obviously would add that cost to the location rental fee.

Their Big Day is *Your* 3- to 5-Day Event

Weddings generally are held on the "big day" and some traditions entail wedding celebrations lasting over a two-day period. However, from your perspective, weddings are a 3- to 5-day event. A day or two prior to the wedding ceremony, you'll need to receive delivery of the furniture rentals, tents, and other setup items.

Tents and basic decorations may be set up two days before the wedding itself so that they'll be in place for any rehearsal that may take place the day before the wedding. Also the band may want to rehearse or do a preliminary sound check the day before the wedding.

Then the day after the event itself, the various rentals are picked up and the property is cleaned and restored to its original condition. If the wedding is held on a Saturday, the pick-up and cleaning may not occur until Monday. So you could end up with a 5-day use of your property, during which time you would not be able to rent it out to another group.

Since a wedding is such a special day, the preparations may take longer than you think. You'll want your property polished and pretty. A visual check the week prior may reveal a broken sprinkler to be fixed, a dead bush to be removed, or the BBQ and countertop that didn't get cleaned after your last cookout. There are no re-takes or postproduction for a wedding. So everything has to be right.

Some homeowners generate additional cash from weddings by offering overnight rooms to the out-of-town guests coming for the wedding. Since these guests would otherwise have to book rooms in expensive nearby hotels, they're apt to lodge with you if you can offer a room or two at an attractive price. Check out the ins and outs of operating a Bed & Breakfast (#9) or offering a room as a virtual B&B (#10).

Some years ago I interviewed a woman who hosted many large weddings at her huge home overlooking the ocean in Malibu. She told me that she limited the number of weddings to one or two per month mostly during the summer months.

"Every month I'm turning business away," she confided.

"Why stop with 1 or 2 weddings when you could host a wedding every weekend in the summer?" I asked. "You could double your money!"

"Yes," she replied. "But weddings are too intense. It's enough to do one or two." She went on to explain, "We host large weddings and some are two-day events with the extended family participating. It's lucrative for us because we rent rooms to the family for several days but it's exhausting. One wedding a month is enough but sometimes we do two."

Now I understand what the homeowner meant. Weddings can be very intense, indeed! Weddings are all about magic and enchantment on the special day but it takes a lot of work behind the scenes to make it all happen smoothly.

Wedding Location Rentals pay *what*?

Some homeowners charge as they would for a filming project. The main shoot day—in this case, the wedding day itself—pays the full daily rate while the prep and strike days pay up to half of that amount. Therefore, you'll want to charge based on four or even five days of usage rather than a single day. Remember, you won't be able to rent the property to anyone else until the wedding is completely "wrapped."

If your property can accommodate a large wedding of 200 people or more, you may be able to charge up to **$4,000** or more for the location alone. Prestige homes with views in my area garner up to $10,000 and beyond for very large weddings (i.e. over 300 attendees). The pricing depends largely on your area so you should check local listings for the going rates.

In some areas, weddings may be scheduled a year in advance. Again, depending on local norms, you could charge a deposit of up to 50 percent of the full fee at the time of scheduling to book and confirm the date.

To get started, contact a local private venue for weddings that is well established and explore their willingness to refer business to you. During the busy time of the year (i.e. June and the other summer months), they can only book so many weddings before having to turn potential business away. If you offer them the opportunity to capture a piece of that business by partnering with you, it's a win-win situation. You can approach them with the offer of nearby overnight accommodations for the wedding guests. See strategy #9 in this book for information on how to offer your spare rooms as a Bed & Breakfast.

Top Do's & Don'ts for Wedding Location Rentals

• Do specify the timeframe and all other terms in a written contract including the start and end time on the day of the wedding. Then charge a pro-rated hourly fee for overtime.

- <u>Do</u> take pictures of your property, once it's decorated, for later use in marketing your home as a wedding destination. Wedding decorations and lighting can make your property look absolutely enchanting. Don't miss the opportunity to capture the magic on film.
- <u>Do</u> have a contingency plan for bad weather or other unforeseeable circumstances. If you cannot accommodate the event inside your home, then tents and covered walkways may need to be arranged.

- <u>Don't</u> forget to put all the details in writing so there won't be any surprises including cleaning costs and temporary insurance that includes $1,000,000 to $2,000,000 in liability coverage. The insurance certificate should cover the setup days and remain in force until the property is completely restored after the wedding.
- <u>Don't</u> allow rice, confetti, or sparklers unless you want to clean up the mess and risk the liability of a fire. Also check with local authorities on the permissibility of having a fire or sparklers.
- <u>Don't</u> fail to plan for crowd management and parking. It may fall to you to provide valet parking attendants; if so, you'll need to include that expense in the location fee. Decide whether or not you want guests to have the run of your home. If not, there will need to be a rest room accessible from the outside for guests.

Chapter Three. Short-term Rentals & Boarders

Some of these rentals require you to move out of your home temporarily and others do not. In the previous chapter, you discovered that many producers pay you a relocation stipend, above and beyond the rental income, when the location rental requires a takeover of your home. In contrast, the types of rentals discussed in this chapter require you to build your cost of relocation, if needed, into the rental rate.

There is another key difference between some of the rental ideas in this chapter and film location rentals discussed in the previous chapter. Some of these ideas fall under tenant-landlord laws so if you move out of your home and provide keys to a tenant, it's advisable to exercise extreme caution in selecting the tenant. It's advisable to seek the services of a real estate agent, local landlord group, attorney or other professional who can check a prospective tenant's credit and background. In some areas, landlords now can obtain rent default insurance if they've thoroughly checked out the tenant. Personally, I would never rent out a property to tenants without this type of insurance now that it is available in my area.

7. *Rent out your fully furnished home short-term.*

Need to generate cash fast with minimal investment? If you have an inexpensive place to stay temporarily (i.e. at your relatives, with a neighbor, or on a low-budget vacation), you could rent out your house fully furnished for a month or more as a short-term furnished residential lease for more money than you might have imagined.

Big Demand + Little Supply = More Cash for You

There is a strong and growing demand today for short-term rentals as I discovered when my family needed to relocate during a 2-month film location rental of our home. Initially unconcerned due to the seemingly ample funds we received for relocation, I was aghast to find absolutely no vacancies in the extended-stay hotels within a reasonable drive from our home…in the middle of a major recession!

As it turns out, many families now move to extended-stay hotels after losing a home to foreclosure or after selling in order to downsize. Add that extra demand to the ongoing demand for temporary housing and the supply just can't keep up, which is where you come in.

The advantages your home offers over the extended-stay hotels are many. For one thing your home is probably much larger since most of those hotel rooms are less than 1,000 square feet. In addition, your home may have an attached garage, private laundry room, and private back yard.

There may also be some disadvantages from the tenants' point of view. You probably won't offer daily maid service, free breakfasts, other meals and snacks, front desk or concierge service. Also your home may not have the extensive amenities found at the extended stay hotels such as a pool, spa, workout room, basketball court and so on.

Stop by a local extended-stay hotel or research them online to see how your home would compare: Marriott Residence Inn (*Marriott.com*), Extended Stay America (*extendedstayamerica.com*), or Homestead Suites (*homesteadhotels.com*).

Short-term Rentals pay *what?*

After checking out the rates in your area for a suite in an extended-stay hotel, you'll have a better idea what alternatives the prospective tenant faces. In my area, for example, a 2-room suite at the Marriott Residence Inn is about $175 per night with taxes. That figure amounts to over $5,000 per month! You could undercut the commercial guys by 20 percent and still charge $4,000 per month. If that amount sounds astronomical compared with leasing rates of homes in your area, remember that you would be providing the short-term rental fully furnished and live-in ready. The rate needs to cover all utilities including television and Internet service. The tenants will bring only their toothbrushes and clothing.

It is informative to look at long-term rental rates for homes in your area as well as rates for local apartments available on a short-term basis. Some of these properties may claim to be "furnished" but realize that they probably are not "live-in ready." After moving in, the renter must arrange for the utilities, order television and phone service, set up Internet service, furnish the kitchen, and so much more.

In contrast, if you provide your home with most of these amenities already in place, your renters can move in as they would with an extended-stay hotel so you should charge accordingly. As a very rough rule of thumb, consider charging 50 to 100 percent more than what your home would be worth as a long-term rental. So if homes in your area rent for $2,000 per month unfurnished as a 12-month rental, you could price your turnkey short-term rental at $3,000 to $4,000 per month.

Check with Zillow (*zillow.com*) as explained in strategy #51 to determine the approximate rental value of your home as a long-term lease (i.e. 12 months or more). Then adjust for the added benefits of a short-term lease that is fully furnished down to the linens and flatware, all utilities hooked up and included in the rental rate, TVs and internet in place and ready to use etc.

Top Do's and Don'ts for Short-term Rentals

- <u>Do</u> consider using a reputable local Realtor who will check the credit and background of a prospective tenant, collect an ample security deposit, and make sure your interests are protected with a written lease agreement. Also check whether there is rent default insurance available for your area and for short-term rentals (a 3-month minimum lease is required in my area).
- <u>Do</u> remove or lock up many of your personal items and remove your valuables to a safe deposit box. Install locks on several cabinets and drawers, lock your garage storage cabinets, and place a deadbolt lock on an extra closet or two so you don't have to move all of your personal belongings.
- <u>Do</u> leave the basic furnishings and décor, creature comforts, books, tapes, bedding, kitchen utensils, TVs, Internet modem, cleaning materials etc. Remove (or lock up) your clothing, personal computers, paperwork, and food from your frig and freezer except for condiments like salt, spices and the like.

- <u>Don't</u> undercharge by basing your monthly rent on the going rate for long-term rentals. The rent has to cover the utilities and allow for wear and tear on the furnishings as well as on the house. For a three-month or longer rental by a large family, it may behoove you to put the electricity in the tenant's name or require that they pay the utility bills as they become due.
- <u>Don't</u> forego an adequate security deposit since your furniture and belongings could be damaged in addition to the house itself. Check with a local Realtor regarding the laws affecting limits on security deposits in your state or locale. In my area, you can collect three times the monthly rental rate as a security deposit for a furnished home although the reality is that it's difficult to get a short-term renter to pay a deposit that large.
- <u>Don't</u> fail to check on local ordinances governing short-term rentals. If you're using a local Realtor, he or she should be aware of any such rules. In my area, for example, there are special local taxes on rentals shorter than 30 days.

8. Secure cash upfront for vacation rentals.

You can take advantage of lucrative vacation rentals whether or not you reside in a stereotypic vacation destination. The reason lies in the fact that vacationers want to "get away" and seek something different than what they experience every day. City dwellers seek out homes in the countryside; beach dwellers go to the mountains; country folks vacation in the city. So virtually no matter where you live, someone will see your home as a vacation getaway.

Cheaper and Better than Hotels

Increasingly, vacationers today opt for renting private homes as they seek more privacy, more space and oftentimes more amenities than they find at a hotel. According to one vacation rental company, the average size of a vacation rental property is 1,850 square feet whereas the average size of a hotel room is 325 square feet.[7] Hotels can be noisy with overcrowded pools and extra charges for many of the amenities. In contrast, private vacation rentals offer a greater level of peace and privacy.

On average, vacation rentals run about 50 percent less expensive per square foot than hotels.[8] In some popular destinations, hotels cost travelers 80 percent more per square foot than private vacation rentals in those locations.

Homeowners are signing up with vacation rental agencies in droves. One top company reports that it's adding 15,000 new properties to its website every month. That company further reports that about 20 percent of the homeowners signing up to rent out their property as a vacation rental do so because of economic hardship.[9]

As a homeowner considering vacation rentals, it helps to visit a local hotel near your home to see what they offer. While you're there, be sure to take a sampling of brochures on display in the lobby for the main attractions in your area. Besides sharing these brochures with your guests, you probably will be amazed at how many fun activities your area offers to vacationers. Reading these brochures will help you get into a vacation mindset. Then you can communicate more effectively with prospective renters.

"Will it play in Peoria?"

The phrase "Will It Play in Peoria?" refers to the idea that if something works or is popular in the Peoria test market, it will be popular nationwide. As a vacation destination, I've never considered Central Illinois near Peoria as offering much appeal. So if Peoria could attract tourists, then just about anywhere in the U.S. should be successful for vacation rentals.

During a trip to Central Illinois about a year ago, I encountered a problem trying to book a room there. Most of the hotels were full! I discovered that the reason they were packed was that the hotels were located near a local riverboat casino that draws visitors from all over the region. The floating casino consists of a large boat on the Mississippi River, where legalized gambling occurs outside of the state's official boundaries.

I eventually did find a room there and while waiting for the elevator one evening, I pulled a tourist brochure off the rack. The display included brochures for dozens of sightseeing opportunities in the surrounding area: tourist-friendly orchards and farms, Abraham Lincoln historic sites, state and national parks, sports facilities and events, local festivals and more. It turns out that vacationers *flock* to the Peoria area almost year around! Yes, vacationing "plays in Peoria" and can work for your area too. When you start looking at your own locale through the eyes of a visitor, you may be surprised at its tourist appeal for vacationers.

Succeeding with Vacation Rentals

Vacation rentals share some similarities to short-term rentals but there are important differences. For both types of rentals, your own family needs to relocate while renting out your home for a profit. Can you stay with relatives, rent your neighbor's RV, or go on a camping trip?

You'll find a variety of websites to help you succeed with vacation rentals. Some sites serve only as the matchmaker and let you take it from there. Others do the booking and collection of rents for you.

The matchmaking sites typically charge you an annual fee to list your property on the site. Then when prospects click a desired destination, they can see pictures of your specific property that you've posted. If they like what they see online, they can contact you (or your agent) directly for availability, rates and booking.

Dealing directly with the owner or agent provides more intimate information regarding the vacation home and its features," explains one vacation rental site, "leading to a more enjoyable vacation" for the travelers.[10] As the homeowner, you have the opportunity to talk directly with the prospective visitors and answer any questions they may have.

Some sites require that you pass a screening process and they use a third-party servicer specializing in security to do the screening. Even with well-screened affiliates, sometimes things go wrong and it helps allay vacationers' fears if the vacation rental matchmaker offers a guarantee or insurance. One of the largest vacation rental communities offers thousands of dollars in a guarantee to travelers if it turns out the home has been foreclosed, double-booked, or simply is not as advertised.

Check *CashCowCasa.com*, the companion website of this book, to find links to top vacation rental sites. You could register your home with one of these services and begin getting bookings sooner than you think since the vacation rental matchmakers let you offer "last minute" specials to attract travelers.

Turn Your Property into a Virtual Timeshare

As you make contact with folks coming to rent your place as a vacation rental, consider approaching them with the prospect of a recurring rental in future years. Assuming the travelers love your place and want to return again in the future, offer a discounted rate for booking the next two or three years in advance. If they'll only commit to a year, grant them the rights to rent your place at a certain time next year. Call it a "virtual timeshare" so it gives them a feeling of ownership of the property.

Whatever future bookings you arrange, you'll be able to collect a portion of the rental fee upfront when you ink the deal and then collect the remaining rent when they arrive for each year's vacation.

Vacation Rentals pay *what?*

Vacation rental rates bring in more on a per night basis than short-term residential rentals. According to a survey conducted by HomeAway.com, owners registered with their site who rent their second homes make, on average, more than **$33,000 a year** in rental revenue![11]

In order to determine what you'll need to charge to make money, first you have to determine your costs. Total up the average monthly utility costs, property taxes, and mortgage-related costs (including principal, interest, taxes and insurance—referred to as PITI). Multiplying by 12 gives you the approximate annual costs.

The next step is to determine how much you can charge for your property as a vacation rental. You can start by looking online at the vacation rental sites in your area to see how your home compares with others offered for rent. Also check with your local real estate agent.

It helps to familiarize yourself with local hotel rates in your area including long-term rates for suites at the extended-stay hotels. Rates will vary by season in most locations. *High season* generally occurs during the summertime when vacationers have time to travel whereas the *low season* often occurs during winter months unless you live in an area that offers venues for winter sports. Use the seasonal rates at your local extended-stay hotels as a guide for how much you may have to discount your rates during the off season.

Based on the industry average, you would charge about 50 percent less than the hotels. However if your geographical area is a preferred vacation destination and the hotels are mostly filled, you may be able to charge a higher percentage such as 75 percent of the going hotel rate.

Some of the major vacation rental sites offer ROI (return on investment) calculators that help you figure out how many weeks you would need to rent your place to break even on your expenses. Then you'll know how much you'll have to rent your place to go beyond the basic costs of ownership.

Top Do's and Don'ts for Vacation Rentals

- Do register with a highly regarded vacation rental site that allows user reviews to help build your positive reputation as a trusted vacation site. In your marketing description, let prospective renters know that your home has high-speed Internet access and cell phone reception. For many travelers, it's a deal breaker if you don't have those services.
- Do check with your local authority to see if there is a vacation rental sales tax in your area. Find out if you'll need to register your property, how much sales tax you should collect, and when you'll need to make tax payments. These taxes may range from 5 to 15 percent tax on the total rental fees.
- Do share a written inventory of your basic kitchen contents so the renters will know what to expect and won't have to barrage you with emails asking, "Is there a BBQ? Blender? Garlic press? Microwave oven? Toaster? Muffin tins? Slow cooker? Juicer?" The list also helps keep the guests honest. If you have a collection of DVDs, you can also provide an inventory list for those. By the way, it's a nice gesture to provide a "Forgot something?" basket of travel-sized toiletries. Let the guests know about the basket in case they forgot to bring any of these items.

- Don't lose prospective guests who you have to turn away during the high season such as summer vacation once you're already booked. Offer them a weekend, week, or month during the "low season" at a more favorable rate.

- <u>Don't</u> leave your old towels or used bars of soap in the bathrooms. Guests will be impressed if you provide large fluffy white towels and fresh new soaps or full soap containers.
- <u>Don't</u> leave guests in a lurch during an emergency. Provide an "Operations Manual" for the home that has a section explaining emergency procedures such as the location of electric panels and water main shut off. Also provide an "Emergency Kit" in a box or basket that contains a first aid kit, flashlights, extra batteries, a wind-up radio, lighter, fire extinguisher and other items relevant to emergencies that could arise in your area.

9. Monetize spare rooms with a Bed & Breakfast.

The advantages of running a B&B are many according to one major B&B site and include, "having the freedom to choose which 20 hours a day you'd like to work."[12]

Consider turning your home into a B&B if you enjoy meeting people, your house has a certain charm or beauty, you or another adult in the family is home much of the time, and you have two or more spare bedrooms. Travelers seek out B&Bs in busy cities, small town neighborhoods, popular tourist destinations, and peaceful country settings.

B&B establishments sound very European but have become popular in the U.S. as an alternative to hotels. While B&Bs may charge a little less than hotels, many travelers prefer B&Bs to hotels not so much for any cost savings but for the opportunity to experience the local ambiance and culture up close. B&Bs provide travelers the chance to interact with locals (i.e. You!) on a personal basis.

B&Bs compete directly with hotels and often win. According to a recent survey, most travelers (71%) say B&Bs provide more value than hotels. Travelers cite the free breakfasts, free parking, wireless Internet service and other amenities. Most travelers surveyed (84%) said they would choose a B&B over a hotel if both were priced at the same daily rate.[13]

Most B&Bs share a common set of attributes that travelers appreciate. Most inns are owner-operated and independent, not part of a chain. The available rooms in a B&B are individually decorated and have a distinctive "theme" so that travelers, for example, can select between the "African Safari" room and the "Beachside Cottage" room.

Breakfast is provided by the innkeeper and may consist of simple *continental* faire left out for guests or a more elaborate offering such as quiche or homemade breakfast specialties. Finally, an inn should include a common area where guests can gather such as a family room, recreation room, living room, or lounge.

What's Required to Become a B&B

A leading B&B site claims that it generates over $85 million in annual reservations for its member properties. Here are the site's requirements for owners who want to register as a B&B establishment on its site:

- Furnish the rooms you offer for rent with different themes or decor;
- Provide some type of breakfast if only pastries and juice;
- Offer nightly rental rates.

You'll need to ready your home so that it works well as an inn both for the guests and for your family. First, each bedroom offered for rent should have a keyed lock so that guests can come and go, as they like. It helps if the common area and rented rooms could be separated from the rest of your home. A strategically placed interior door and a few locked cabinets and closet doors can do wonders to preserve your privacy (and security).

Nearly all B&Bs today offer private baths in some, if not all, rooms. If your extra bedrooms do not have private baths and guests would have to share a bathroom, your rates would have to be lower but your B&B would appeal to travelers looking to economize. According to industry statistics, approximately 12 percent of B&B rooms have a shared bathroom.

Upscale B&Bs are increasingly popular with travelers who want 5-star accommodations and service at an affordable price. These full-service B&Bs offer special amenities such as afternoon teas, wine and cheese hours, private pools, spas and spa services, luxury soaps and personal care products, high thread-count linens, and more. If you want to go the upscale route, you'll have to be professionally inspected and maintain positive reviews from clients.

Listing Your Home with a B&B Service

If you're serious about making money as a B&B, it's well worth it to list your home with one of the major B&B websites (check the companion site *CashCowCasa.com* for links to current sites). There are several large B&B sites that will list and promote your property to travelers looking for B&Bs in your area. If you have your own website, a B&B service can route prospective guests to your website or the service can handle all bookings and payments for you.

Some B&B services give you the option to list your B&B rooms on the major international travel sites such as *Expedia.com*, *hotels.com*, and *Travelocity.com*. The reason it's so helpful to have international exposure on these major travel sites is that over 70 percent of travel reservations are made online with most of those reservations made on the top travel sites. Finding your rooms on a leading travel site will allow travelers to either book online or contact you directly.

B&B's pay *what?*

The difference between B&B rates and hotel rates may be negligible so check out the going room rates in your area. Remember that a B&B offers advantages over a typical hotel: local ambiance, homey accommodations, and homemade or fresh breakfast faire, to name a few.

Registering your property with a leading B&B site gives you the visibility you need to keep your rooms rented. One of the leading B&B sites reports that their top-level members average 129 room-nights rented per year. Assuming your room has a private bath and you offer various amenities for an "upscale" stay, you could charge $125 per night (before taxes) or more if the hotel rates in your area support that amount. Those figures translate to a target annual income of **$16,125**.

You could boost your rates by combining overnight stays with other services such as providing a wedding venue. See tip #6 for ideas about how to partner with leading wedding venues in your area to capture their overflow business.

You'll have to decide whether you want the B&B service to handle all reservations and payments or if you want to gear up to handle that for yourself. Realize that most of the B&B servicers don't actually pay you until after the guests have arrived and possibly until after they've left. It's good to read the fine print so you know what to expect.

Top Do's and Don'ts for B&Bs

- <u>Do</u> learn about the B&B business before jumping in: Talk to innkeepers, read books, check out the many free online guides, and become a B&B guest at a well-established inn to see how it all works. It's hard to be a good innkeeper if you've never experienced the hospitality of a good innkeeper yourself.
- <u>Do</u> represent your B&B listing accurately in ads and marketing materials. Let prospective guests see the rooms and surroundings truthfully and be frank about expectations, rules, pricing, and amenities.

- <u>Do</u> affiliate with a B&B website that promotes you to the major international travel sites (i.e. Expedia, Travelocity etc.) if you're serious about filling your B&B rooms.

- <u>Don't</u> rely solely on a B&B website to promote your rooms. Most travelers will never visit a B&B website because they perceive B&Bs as lacking privacy and think they'll have to share a bathroom, both of which are myths. Only 12 percent of B&B rooms share bathroom facilities and the privacy factor of today's B&B far exceeds privacy found at most hotels.
- <u>Don't</u> cancel reservations since travelers depend on you for a smooth travel itinerary. In a true emergency, contact your B&B website servicer since they may be able to help find a last-minute replacement.
- <u>Don't</u> waste money purchasing new items for themed rooms; gather 5 or 6 related items you already own that suggest a theme (such as Safari, Seashore, Hawaiian, Country, Old West, 50's Music etc) then complete the room with neutral furnishings in theme-related or neutral colors.

10. Add to your coffers with a "Virtual B&B."

Running a true Bed & Breakfast inn admittedly takes time, money, and several spare bedrooms. If your time is limited and you have only one spare guest room or bedroom, you could run a "virtual B&B." An enterprising young company, Airbnb, serves as an eBay equivalent that provides a marketplace for hosts and travelers to match up and transact business. As a room host, Airbnb enables you to reach out to the world to find a traveler who will pay handsomely for your spare room. Bookings have been growing at about 40 percent per month[14] and rival the number of rooms offered by major hotel chains such as Hilton Hotels.

"We've made a huge contribution to saving a whole bunch of homes," said one of Airbnb's founders, who receives hundreds of e-mails from people turning to the site as a way to stave off foreclosure. "There were so many people who just couldn't pay their mortgage and couldn't sell their home."[15] The site is full of success stories from homeowners who have stayed afloat thanks to renting out extra rooms. By the way, the site can also help you rent out a boat if you have one.

Here's how the process works:
- Hosts like yourself list for free by completing a profile, uploading photos, naming a price, and setting availability using the site's online calendar.

- Reservation requests come through the site's online messaging system. Once you receive a reservation request, you can either accept or decline it. If you accept, you can contact your guest directly to confirm details. The site collects and later distributes rental payments.
- Finally, you'll be paid 24 hours after check in. Both host and guest issue an online review of one another on the Airbnb site, resulting in feedback ratings similar to user ratings on eBay.

Safeguards and Trust Building

The system of reviews for both hosts and travelers is designed to keep the process safe for all parties. Everyone has a profile that can be shared. As a host, you can see a user's history on Airbnb, giving you more insight about a potential guest. You'll see if a user has verified their phone number, connected their Facebook account, and whether the majority of their reviews are positive.

The Airbnb site attempts to boost trust through social networking. With millions of bookings already, the chances are that someone in a guest's network may have already used Airbnb. So guests can feel more comfortable (and vice versa) if you are in their social network or have other connections such as being from the same alma mater or company.

Couch Surfing, Anyone?

The Airbnb website allows hosts to offer a couch for a nightly rate. In other words, you could rent out the couch in your living room to a traveler willing to sleep on the couch and share bathroom facilities. Browsing through the Airbnb site reveals occasional couch offerings for about $25 to $35 per night.

I don't know anyone who has hosted a traveler on the family couch and must say that it sounds weird if not downright scary. However, due to the many safeguards in place for screening potential guests, it could be perfectly safe. If you've ventured into renting out your couch, please share your story on our website at *CashCowCasa.com* and give us a shout out with your "Moolah Moo."

Virtual B&B's pay *what?*

Realize that your prospective guests are looking to save money by staying in a private home rather than in a hotel or established B&B. You'll need to charge significantly less than either of these alternatives so begin by researching how much guests have to pay for a local hotel room or for accommodations at a B&B inn.

Your best bet is to sound as much like a local B&B as possible yet charge a lower rate. It helps if your room has its own private bathroom and you provide an appealing breakfast such as homemade muffins and local fruit along with coffee and tea.

In my area, homeowners are getting up to $100 per night or higher especially if you coordinate with nearby inns and venues for weddings and other special events. During busy times, these establishments can send you their overflow.

One woman turned to renting out rooms when she lost her job after being relocated to the Washington D.C. area. She was in the process of buying a house when her company decided not to expand due to the recession. By renting out a room as a virtual B&B, she was able to pull in more than **$13,000** in a year, renting the room for about $115 per night.[16]

Top Do's and Don'ts for Virtual B&Bs

- Do require a complete profile of a guest before accepting a booking. At the Airbnb site, you can block booking requests by guests who do not meet certain criteria or who don't have complete profiles (similar to setting minimum buyer criteria on eBay). Expect to pay the company a fee of about 3 percent of the rental amount.
- Do update your spare room's online availability calendar frequently and return inquiries promptly. Too busy this week to be bothered with guests? Just block out those dates on the calendar. When guests do arrive for check in on the days you're available, be ready with a smile.
- Do collect a security deposit to cover accidents and mishaps, like a broken lamp or some spilled wine. Check with Airbnb about their current insurance protection for damages caused from theft or vandalism by a guest.

- Don't fail to ask a guest about the purpose of the trip. It might affect your decision to rent your spare room if you know the guest is coming to your city to attend a convention or if the guest is moving to your city to find a new job.
- Don't rely on your own photos of your bedroom or other space that you offer for rent. You're better off to have "verified photos" which means a professional Airbnb photographer visits your property, captures the right shots, and then uploads great-looking photos for you.
- Don't give your room guests the run of your home when you're not there. It's better to install an inexpensive door strategically placed between the spare room and the main part of your house if possible.

11. Bring in steady cash-flow from a roommate.

Renting out a room to a quiet single or student may not pay as much per night as a virtual B&B but longer-term room rentals can be a great way to generate a consistent cash flow from an extra bedroom that you rarely use. Do you have a guest room that sits unused most of the time? Why not add a sofa bed to your family room, or other area, for occasional guests and turn your guest room into a cash generator!

Decisions, Decisions, Decisions

It's a good idea to put everything in writing once you decide what rules to establish. Also spell out the consequences to breaking the rules.

Smoking or Non-smoking? Some homeowners rent to smokers but restrict smoking to outside only. One homeowner allowed outdoor smoking but had one roommate whose clothes reeked so badly of smoke that it brought the smell indoors. When the heat or air conditioning kicked on, he could smell the smoke from the roommate's clothes throughout the house.

Furnished or Unfurnished? It can be a big selling point to offer a room furnished. College students and others moving in from out of state can rent a room furnished and not worry about moving or renting furniture. One homeowner explained that they were able to borrow some furniture and buy the rest inexpensively so it cost them less than $200 to furnish two rooms.

Pets or No pets? You may have pets in your home, but do you want to add the complication of your roommate's pets trying to get along with your pets? If you do decide to complicate your life with a roommate's pet, you may want to check out helpful products such as feline pheromones that calm down confrontational cats, for example.

Guests or No Guests? You need to decide ahead of time at what point your tenant's guest becomes an additional tenant and make that rule clear in writing. If your tenant has someone sleeping over four nights a week, you now have two tenants using your premises and utilities, but only one is paying.

Room & Board or Room only? If you value your privacy, you may want to provide a separate entrance to the rented room and keep your life separate from that of your tenant. Obviously, the room would have to have its own bathroom, small frig, microwave oven, and sitting area. If you don't mind sharing your home, offering board expands the number of prospective people that you'll consider as well as the amount you can charge. Either way you'll want to advertise the rental rate without the board costs and quote those separately.

Use of Kitchen/laundry facilities or not? Here's where it helps to spell out the specifics upfront. If you allow the tenant to use your laundry facilities, agree to a specific day or time for the use. One homeowner believed that a tenant was taking in other people's laundry since she was using the washer and dryer constantly. Limit hours for kitchen access or you could hear pots and pans banging at 2:00 am.

Flat rate or Prorated utilities? You'll need to decide whether to prorate the utilities or roll the anticipated usage increase into a flat rental rate. There are proponents and opponents of each approach. Some homeowners complain that prorating utilities is a hassle since bills arrive at different times and it's hard to quantify the proration. Others report getting burned when charging a flat rate. For example, one homeowner rented a room with utilities to a male college student who did not overuse the utilities but his visiting girlfriend did. A workable approach for some has been to quote a total flat rate that consists of a base rent plus an estimated average utility allowance (i.e. Rent of $500/mo consists of $450 base + $50 utilities) and agree that the tenant will pay an additional prorated amount if the utility use goes overboard significantly.

Take Precautions, Check with Experts, Boost Income

Families with children should require a background check for anyone living in or around their property. Nowadays, it's standard practice for adults to get clearance before working around children. Even volunteers in schools and sports teams must be checked out. Have your agent or landlord organization run a background check on any prospective tenant or roommate.

Check with your accountant about the tax implications of renting a portion of your home. You may need to report the rental income on your tax return and your home will be considered a rental property. Since you live in the home, you might not be able to report a rental "loss" in the same way you could with a separate rental property.

Delivering special services to boarders can boost your rental income if you have special knowledge and skills. Do you or a family member have a nursing degree or medical experience? You could boost your rental income by serving special-needs groups such as the elderly or boarders needing a place to recuperate. Perhaps you are a nutritionist or a fabulous gourmet cook. These skills expand the range of services that you could provide. Check on state and local licensing requirements for delivering special services in your area.

Hooking Up with a Roommate

One popular service called iRoommates allows you to enter a basic listing at no cost but does charge for using their database of prospective roommates. The benefit of paying the fee and gaining access to their database is that you can contact "tenant matches" consisting of prospective tenants who match your criteria. It's a way to speed up the process of finding a suitable boarder. Rather than waiting passively to be found by tenants, you actively reach out to prospective roommates. In just a few minutes, you can send thousands of emails to a select group of prospective tenants.

Prefer college students? Advertising for a graduate student sends the message that you're looking for a quiet tenant, not a party animal. There are special websites that let you advertise for students. I know a number of homeowners, including myself, who have had success by posting rental listings on student-oriented sites. There are companies that run the off-campus housing service for partner schools so they understand how best to service college students, schools, and landlords. Check our companion website at *CashCowCasa.com* for resources to help you connect with a roommate.

Room Rentals pay *what?*

Compared with renting out your room as a virtual B&B, a long-term room rental could generate more cash over the long run since it provides consistent income. In contrast, virtual B&Bs may pay more per night but your total intake will depend on how often the room is rented versus how often it sits empty. As online services for short-term room rentals gain popularity and trust, you may have the option of having an uninterrupted series of short-term roommates versus one semi-permanent roommate.

Check out local rates in your area for roommates on one of the roommate sites and see how your room fits in. In many areas, you can get $500 to $600 per month for a room rental including utilities. In cities and popular areas, it's likely to be double those numbers.

Top Do's and Don'ts for Room Rentals
- <u>Do</u> put everything in writing. It helps to consult with an appropriate professional. A real estate agent, for example, can help with a rental

agreement, tenant screening, and local requirements such as whether you need to install smoke and carbon monoxide detectors, a good idea even if not officially required.

- <u>Do</u> attract a good tenant with favorable descriptions of your room for rent including cable TV and wireless Internet. Follow Fair Housing practices when you advertise and interview prospective tenants. If you're not sure what you can say and not say, seek assistance from a licensed local Realtor who has had training in Fair Housing procedures.
- <u>Do</u> protect yourself from identity theft prior to bringing a roommate into your home. Consider renting a P.O. box and receiving your bills and other mail there. Add locks to your bedroom and closet doors. Also keep papers in a locked file and rent a bank safe deposit box to store sensitive documents and keepsakes.

- <u>Don't</u> squeeze every cent of rent from a tenant. Many successful landlords have told me that they deliberately undercharge so that they have their pick of tenants.
- <u>Don't</u> forget to spell out all rules ahead of time. Will you allow smoking, pets, parties, noise after 10 pm, parking, and overnight guests? Also be frank about the consequences if rules are broken—i.e. fail to cleanup after using the kitchen and lose kitchen privileges for a week.
- <u>Don't</u> fall for scams especially from international "students" who send a cashiers check for too much (with some plausible excuse for the excessive amount) and request that you send back the excess from your account. The bank may "cash" the cashiers check at first but if it's not good they will claw the money back out of your account. Meanwhile, any cash that you sent to "refund" the overage will be gone.

12. Generate income from a makeshift guesthouse.

If you have a guesthouse, you probably have it rented out already. But assuming you don't: "Trailers for sale or rent. Rooms to let...fifty cents." Roger Miller's lyrics may miss the mark pricewise, but you could feel like the king (or queen) of the road if you can turn your trailer, RV, or backyard cottage into a moneymaker.

<u>Instant "Guesthouse" on a Shoe String Budget</u>

Many RV parks today won't allow coaches over 15 years old, so there are many older but serviceable RVs available for a fraction of the original cost. The situation is similar for older, large travel trailers. If allowed in your area, these older units make fully equipped living quarters if you provide hookups for water, electricity, and waste disposal.

The hookups will require special preparation but it's certainly faster and cheaper than building a guesthouse. You'll need to have an electrician install 50-amp electric service, which allows an RV's round dryer-type plug to connect to the 3-prong outlet. The water hookup can run off of an existing water spigot in your yard (although the special connection hose is higher quality than a standard garden hose). The waste water/sewer hookup requires a plumber to tap into the septic or sewer system, which most likely will require a permit.

You may need to add a coat of paint to the exterior of the unit especially if it's older. Then finish things off with some pretty flowers, bushes, and potted plants around the unit to make it feel homier. A parking area will also be needed nearby.

Guesthouse Rentals pay *what?*

Visit *Zillow.com* and type in your home address to see property values in your local area. By checking just the "For Rent" box, a map will display small markers for each available rental in your area. You should be able to quickly determine the starting rates for apartments along with rates for small homes. Note the square footage of the listed rentals and compare with your guesthouse. If your rental is substantially smaller, it will need to be priced accordingly.

In my area, for example, the going rates for apartments are $1200 to $2000 per month and up, small homes start at $3000 per month and higher. A detached "guesthouse" that is a self-contained trailer or RV is priced similar to a small apartment since all the utilities are included along with dedicated parking space and, generally, use of the homeowner's outdoor facilities such as the backyard, BBQ, and pool.

Top Do's & Don'ts for a Guesthouse

- Do have a written rental agreement and conduct a background/credit check on the prospective tenants. Ask for personal references and check them out.
- Do provide parking next to the guesthouse if feasible. Or provide a designated parking area for the tenants so they don't end up blocking your garage or taking your parking space.
- Do collect a security deposit to cover any damages caused by the tenant. If your property is on a septic system, you may want to collect the equivalent of two months rent as security since damage to the septic system can be costly to repair.

- <u>Don't</u> forget to factor in anticipated utility costs into the monthly rental rate. Since you might not be able to meter the electricity and water separately to the guesthouse, the tenants' utility usage will increase your bill.
- <u>Don't</u> allow a long-term tenant to piggyback on your Internet, cable, or phone service. These services can be installed and billed separately to the guesthouse.
- <u>Don't</u> give your tenants the run of your property unless you've agreed to that situation in the lease. It's best to clarify the permitted uses and limitations upfront in writing. May the tenants use the front yard, pool, or play equipment? Will you allow them to have a large backyard BBQ party every weekend or plant a garden? Many problems can be avoided by spelling out the rules upfront.

13. Rent out your garage as a studio or office.

Your garage represents one of the largest areas of your home that most homeowners could live without in a pinch. With some effort and preparation, your garage could appeal to creative types who need studio space—artists, musicians, photographers, and crafters. (In fact, most of us probably know such a person who actually moved into his parents' garage after high school and is still living there in his 30's or 40's! Right?)

<u>Prepare and Be Suggestive</u>
Before you advertise your garage space online or in local papers, clear out the inevitable clutter that collects in garages. This activity itself can produce some quick cash as explained in another chapter. After removing the clutter, it's a good idea to clean and tidy things up by adding a coat of paint, washing the windows, and replacing the light bulbs with brighter lights.

Widen the garage's appeal further, and reap more money, by adding a few touches to suggest the type of use you're trying to attract. Looking to rent to musicians as a practice studio? Hang a music poster, add a music stand, and include a few chairs. Hope to rent it as an office or shipping department? Leave a worktable or desk in the garage, hang a "success" poster on the wall, and place a lamp or in/out tray on the desk. The garage doesn't have to be furnished and ready to use but just suggestive of its new intended purpose.

By the way, if you don't want to expend extra effort or don't want people coming and going frequently, check out the chapter on Storage. There you'll find ideas about how to rent out your garage as extra storage space, which would entail less preparation as well as less traffic to and from your property.

Garage Rentals pay *what?*
The benchmark for this type of rental is the local going rate for commercial business space. If commercial warehouse space in your area rents for $1.00 per square foot per month and your garage measures about 500 square feet, then an equivalent commercial storage space would cost $500 per month.

Realize that commercial warehouse space may include a climate controlled environment (i.e. heating and air conditioning), a private or shared bathroom, and off-street parking. As a private party, can you provide these amenities? If so, then you can ask closer to the commercial benchmark rate. Otherwise, you'll need to discount your rental rate deeply to incentivize prospective renters.

Top Do's & Don'ts of Garage Rentals
- Do have a written agreement and require an application. Ask for references and check them out. It's best to collect a security deposit equivalent to a month's rent in case the renter causes damage such as a broken window or blown electric circuit.
- Do spell out the permitted hours of access. You wouldn't want a band practicing after 10 pm at night or artists arriving at first light. Creative types sometimes do their best work late at night so access limitations may require some negotiation. After you work out mutually agreeable hours, put it in writing so no one gets amnesia.
- Do move your belongings out of the garage into a shed or cabinet, especially items that you need to access on a periodic basis such as gardening equipment and household supplies. Then reserve several locked cabinets inside the garage for long-term storage of your heavy or bulky items like house paint, tools, and building materials.

- Don't allow your renters to stay overnight or you could end up with a tenant living illegally in your garage. Remain especially vigilant if the garage has a bathroom, mini kitchen area, or blinds on the window. If you don't mind a tenant living in your garage (if it's permissible in your area), then you should charge accordingly.
- Don't fail to specify in writing the terms of use as an art studio, music studio, shipping center or whatever you've agreed to so the renter doesn't use your garage for another purpose. You might not object to a different use, but it's important to set the expectations and rules upfront which will be specific to a particular use.
- Don't forget to factor in the cost of utilities when setting the rental amount. Some uses such as band practices or offices draw more electricity than other uses such as painting and crafts. Most renters will

want to bring a small frig and possibly a microwave oven but your agreement should prohibit hot plates, space heaters, and other energy hogs unless you specifically approve them (and check them for safety).

14. Charge well for RV space rentals with hookups.

Does your home have a large back yard or roomy side yard with access from the street or back alley? Could you provide hookups for water and electricity? Many people today are looking for a place to park their recreational vehicle either during their travels or as temporary housing.

You'll need to check local ordinances for permits and other issues involved with providing space rentals for RVs, trailers, or campers. Municipalities in my area, for example, tack on a 12 percent occupancy tax to short-term rental rates. Adding a sewer or septic hookup probably would require a permit from your local building authority. Other modifications to your property might require permits as well. The expense and hassle of readying your property can be well worth it, however, given the lucrative potential for renting space to RVs, camping trailers, or traditional campers.

Preparing Your Property for RVs or Camping Trailers

At a minimum, RVs and camping trailers need hookups for water and electric. Although a standard electric outlet allows power for the RV's lights, it takes a special outlet to provide 30-amp or 50-amp service required by today's RVs. It's best to provide 50-amp service since that's what needed to run an RV's air conditioning unit. If the RV can take only 30 amps, there's an adapter to "step down" 50-amp service to 30 amps, but you can't go the other way. The plug looks like a dryer plug—a large, round plug with 3-flat prongs. An electrician will need to install this type of outlet outside near the RV parking area.

Your side- or backyard most likely already has water spigots. Just hook a drinking-quality hose to the spigot. Most RVs and camping trailers have large holding tanks up to 40 or more gallons for potable (i.e. drinkable) water.

The biggest issue is how to deal with waste. RVs generally have two or more wastewater storage tanks: "black water" tanks that the toilets empty into and "gray water" tanks that store water coming from the sinks and showers. When full, these holding tanks must be drained at "dump stations," a place where raw sewage may be emptied properly. If you are unable to install a hookup to your own sewer or septic system, you can direct the RV owner to the nearest dump station. Check *SaniDumps.com* for a comprehensive list of dump stations nearest you.

No Prep Need for "Boondocking"

If you don't have the time or money to do the needed modifications to your property, you still could take advantage of this opportunity. RVs can go "boondocking" in your yard, which means camping without any hookups such as water, waste disposal, or electricity. RV and trailer campers can last for days if not weeks relying strictly on internal amenities such as battery-powered lights, propane-powered heat, stored water, and the ability to store waste (for later emptying) in large tanks for gray and black water. Of course, you'll receive less money to host boondockers, but it allows you to get started. Then you might be able to provide electricity and WiFi easier than you think.

Variations on the Theme: Offer Camping in Your Yard

Many travelers today go in style in their RV or camping trailer complete with stove, shower, toilet and other amenities. However, there are still groups who enjoy the simplicity of tent camping. If your home is located in a scenic area or near tourist attractions, you could also cater to tent campers.

Over one 4th of July weekend several years ago, my family and I hosted a group of young photographers who camped on our property during their annual gathering to celebrate their craft, share techniques, and have a good time. The group was large and would not fit inside our home so a few people stayed inside the house but most of the participants slept in tents pitched in the yard. I must admit that I had misgivings to the point that we stipulated the rental payment had to be made in cash upfront, no checks. We also insisted that we be allowed to stay at the property over the weekend.

As it turned out, the group did what they said they would do: Hold meetings, share stories and techniques, take a zillion photos, stage some funny photo ops and have great fun. After the event, we read a feature article in a national magazine about one of the organizers who is a prominent up-and-coming photographer. Who knows, maybe we played a small role in helping make the next Ansel Adams or Dorothea Lange.

RV Space Rentals pay *what?*

Check out the nearest commercial RV park for their daily, weekly, and monthly rental rates. Find out about availability; what you really want to know is their vacancy rate and how it varies throughout the year. Also ask about their amenities. Many parks offer sewer and water hookups, coin-operated laundry facilities, postal services, telephone hookups, cable TV service, propane service, and Internet. Some parks offer game rooms and large screen TVs. It helps to know the competition before setting your price.

Commercial daily rates may vary from $30 to $40 depending on the size of the RV, weekly rates from $200 to $275, and monthly from $650 to $750 or more. Electric hookups are included in the daily and weekly rates, but are calculated and added as a separate charge for monthly rentals. In my area, the rates are considerably higher since it's a popular vacation destination. My local RV park also charges additional fees for pets, boats, and extra folks.

You can get a better idea of what you can charge by taking a look at rates on Craigslist.org for private party RV space rentals. Note that most commercial outfits will not rent past 28 to 30 days. So people looking for a longer-term rental may search for private party offerings.

Top Do's & Don'ts for RV Space Rentals

* <u>Do</u> clarify in a written agreement that the space rental is self-contained. No showers, bathrooms or other amenities are being provided unless explicitly stated in the agreement.
* <u>Do</u> provide "guest" wireless Internet access since most campers want to connect to the web and it essentially costs you nothing to provide access. Just check that your wireless web service reaches the spot where the RV will be parked and provide the WiFi guest code.
* <u>Do</u> a full background and credit check for longer-term tenants. Also collect a security deposit as you would with any type of medium- or long-term lease.

* <u>Don't</u> rent space to RVs and trailers that are too old, run down, or unregistered. Otherwise it could look like you're operating a junkyard. Also you don't want an RV breaking down on your property.
* <u>Don't</u> allow the tenant to hookup to your sewer or use your septic as a "dump station" without your supervision to make sure they follow explicit rules. Provide a print out of the step-by-step guide offered by *SaniDumps.com* for RV owners to use a dump station carefully and correctly.
* <u>Don't</u> forego this income opportunity just because you lack the time or funds to provide hookups since RVs can also go "boondocking" on your property with no hookups at all.

Chapter Four. Storage and Parking

Stuff. Stuff. Stuff. As George Carlin observed "Sometimes you gotta move. You gotta get a bigger house. Why? Too much stuff! You gotta put some of your stuff in *storage*. There's a whole industry based on keeping an eye on your stuff!"

One of the fastest and easiest ways to put cash in your pocket is to tap into the fast growing $20 billion dollar self-storage industry. Nearly one in 10 U.S. households currently rent a self-storage unit, an increase of approximately 65 percent in the last 15 years according to the Self Storage Association that provides stats on the industry.[17]

Regardless of where you are located, plenty of people nearby need storage. Commercial facilities lie mostly in suburban areas (52%) with about a third in urban areas and just under a fifth in rural areas according to the Self Storage Association. The going rate overall for these facilities is about $10 per square foot, ranging from $8 to $11 per square foot depending on location and type of storage facility. Those high rates provide an opportunity for homeowners to capture a piece of this storage business by offering far lower rates.

It's worth a few calls to the commercial storage facilities in your local area to learn about their rates and availability. You can go online to learn more about the top storage companies such as *PublicStorage.com* or *CubeSmart.com*. Also check with your local U-Haul since they account for almost 10 percent of self-storage facilities in the U.S. Once you've researched your competition, you're better able to attract customers and charge them accordingly for these services.

15. Rent out your garage as storage space.

Renting out your garage for storage constitutes one of the fastest and easiest ways to bring in some cash. Perhaps you have a 3-car garage but own only two cars. That third space can be converted to cash in the form of a monthly rental to someone who needs storage space.

Prepare and Separate the Space

If your garage is cluttered, you'll need to begin by clearing out your own belongings to make space for the rental. As mentioned earlier, this activity can bring you some quick cash as explained in another chapter.

For the purpose of renting your garage for storage, your garage doesn't have to look perfect. However, it should be "broom clean" (i.e. swept clean with a broom) with all systems working: doors, locks, and lights.

Nearby apartment dwellers might need to store an extra car, motorcycle, boat, or other vehicle. If you live in a more remote area, your neighbors may appreciate the convenience and cost savings of your garage over a commercial self-storage facility located farther away.

For storage rentals, it's best (but not essential) to segregate the space to be rented from any portion of the garage that you will continue to use. If you're renting one bay of a 3-car garage, it's a good idea to erect a wall, however flimsy, between the rented space and the rest of the garage. Many 3-car garages have a double garage door for the two-car portion of the garage and a single door to the third bay so you could separate the spaces with a temporary plywood "wall." Then later you could remove the plywood if you discontinue the rental or decide to sell your home.

Prospective renters of the storage space will want to know the dimensions of the garage and the hours during which they'll have drive-up access. Security is also a consideration. Plan to supply a garage door remote that opens only the rented bay's automatic door opener or a key that opens the lock on a non-motorized door.

Garage Storage Rentals pay *what?*
Check to see how your local rates compare with the national norm for commercial self-storage, which is around $10 to $12 per square foot per year. Once you've looked up commercial rates, you can find rates from private parties in local classified listings or *Craigslist.org*. As a private party, your price will need to be sufficiently below commercial rates to entice a lessee to rent from you instead of a commercial outfit since most tenants would see the commercial storage company as more stable and more likely to offer relevant services and amenities.

The rate that works for you will depend on the unique desirability of your location in the eyes of the prospective renter and the prices charged by the competition.

Top Do's & Don'ts for Garage Storage Rentals

- <u>Do</u> have a written agreement and require an application at a minimum. Some of the top self-storage companies require no credit check, and they lease to tenants on a month-to-month basis with no lease commitment. However, it's better for you if you find a renter willing to sign a lease and pay a security deposit.
- <u>Do</u> spell out the permitted hours of access. For example, you may not want the renter to have access to the garage after 10 pm at night or before 6 am. A local commercial facility in my area is only open from 9:30 am to 6:00 pm. After that, the gate locks and security cameras take over. Be aware that some commercial drive-up facilities offer access 24/7/365.
- <u>Do</u> try to find a long-term tenant so you spend less time finding and qualifying new renters. Check out the credit and background of your lessee as you would with any tenant. Consider using a real estate agent to do the investigation and draw up the lease to protect your interests.

- <u>Don't</u> attempt to comingle your own use of the garage with the renter's use. You wouldn't want the renter to have access to your belongings and vice versa. It's better to close off the renter's space with a wall or partition, however flimsy or minimal it may be. A long vinyl accordion folding door in the standard 80-inch height would suffice to provide the needed separation. Even arranging tall bookcases side-by-side to form a partitioning wall could work at a minimum.
- <u>Don't</u> fail to specify in writing the terms of use as storage so a lessee doesn't use your garage as a practice studio for his 5-piece rock band. Even if you're agreeable with such a use, you would want to prepare the space and charge accordingly for it.
- <u>Don't</u> allow the renter to store any dangerous or flammable substances and disclose that you'll be keeping an extra remote or key available in case of emergency. Also, let the renter know whether or not the garage is climate controlled since it could affect what can be stored there.

16. Sell parking by the day, week, or month.

Most of us have a love affair with the automobile… until we reach our destination, that is. Then we can't wait to ditch that ride and get on with our day.

Are you a city dweller? Do you live within walking distance of a popular destination? If so, you could get paid to allow drivers to park in your driveway, garage, or parking spot. You're probably a good candidate for parking rentals if:

- You live near a park.
- You live near a school.
- You live near an office building.
- You live near a shopping center.

- You live near a public transit station.
- You live near an entertainment or sports complex.
- You live near a tourist attraction or recreational area.

If you do live within walking distance of a popular facility where parking is in high demand but limited supply, you could rent out a parking space for a tidy sum.

Online parking communities have sprung up on the Internet to serve as veritable matchmakers for parking and enable you to rent your spare parking space by hooking you up with drivers who need parking in your area. One of the largest online parking marketplaces was created to "connect home and business owners who would like to earn money from renting their space with drivers in need of a convenient, safe and cost-effective place to park." The company manages the entire booking process and all the payments so you can be confident that you'll be paid. Check the companion website for this book *CashCowCasa.com* for current matchmaking websites for parking.

Parking Is a Growing Problem

We've all heard about "road rage" but nobody does "parking rage" better than the lead character Madea in the movie *Madea Goes to Jail* by Tyler Perry. Madea (played by Perry) drives her large, older model car slowly through a crowded Kmart parking lot looking for a parking spot. Just as she finds a space, a lady driving a flashy red convertible zips around Madea and takes the spot. Madea, known for her anger management issues, tries to keep her cool in getting the woman to do the right thing, but the woman refuses to give up the parking space and goes into the store.

Madea takes matters into her own hands, literally, as she commandeers a nearby forklift to forcibly move the red car out of "her" space. The car's driver runs out of the store and demands that Medea put the car down so Medea dumps the late model car from the forklift onto the pavement upside down. The driver happens to be married to a police officer and the ensuing events give the movie its title.

The parking scene in the *Madea* movie is hilarious but everyday parking hassles aren't so amusing. As a driver yourself, you probably have experienced the growing problem of parking. Compared with parking in past years, many of us probably have experienced longer waits for a parking space when we go shopping, higher parking fees at work and special events, and higher parking fines for parking misdeeds. (Like I told my CPA, "Wait, you mean I cannot deduct the cost of my parking tickets on Schedule C? I got them in the course of doing business!") Parking is becoming harder to find, far more costly, and downright stressful.

Parking Communities to the Rescue

While the parking problem has grown, many parking spaces and garages sit empty. What's been missing and needed is a way to bring drivers who need to park their vehicles together with property-owners who would love to be paid for their unused garages and parking spaces.

Enter the founder of ParkatmyHouse who saw the problem and brainstormed the solution during a trip to San Francisco. He was on his way to the AT&T stadium in San Francisco to watch a Giants baseball game. As any sports fan knows, trying to find a parking space near a stadium on a game day is virtually impossible! When he noticed an empty driveway a stone's throw away from the stadium, he realized that there was an opportunity for both homeowners and drivers if only they could find a way of making the initial contact with one another. A few months later, his website aimed at connecting people seeking parking with people having parking space to spare opened to the public.

The community approach uses a feedback and review system that has proven so successful on eBay and other communities. As the community becomes more established, members gain a reputation that others in the community can rely on when either booking a parking space or renting out a space. Each party wants peace of mind and assurance that the transaction will be successful and that's the role of the middleman, the parking community website.

Listing your parking space for rent is free. The site charges a commission when they successfully rent it out. You can type in your location at their website along with the type of parking space you have available (i.e. private garage, shared driveway etc.) and receive an estimate of what you could charge for short-term or long-term parking.

No More Parking Rage

Everyone wins when people connect up through a parking matchmaker website. Homeowners are happy when they convert unused space into cash. Drivers are happy when they find low-cost convenient solutions to the ever-increasing price yet shortage of parking. And local businesses win if shoppers don't avoid their smaller shops due to limited parking and opt instead for those big box stores typically surrounded by ample parking.

One winning story came out of the London Olympics from a woman named Diane who used the ParkatmyHouse website to arrange for parking in Ilford, located in the eastern part of Greater London. According to Diane, "We had a five minute walk to Ilford Station and an eight minute train ride to Stratford. Brilliant." [The main Olympic Stadium is located in Stratford, London.]

The perky parker went on to say, "But coming back was even better.....as 80,000 plus spectators headed into central London, we headed back to Ilford on a train with plenty of seats, arrived back to a quiet station and a five minute walk to our car. [The ride home] was quick and smooth. By contrast, other family members chose to catch a train. They missed their last direct train home … because of the delays and ended up … hours later waiting for a connection home. What a great idea this is." Plenty of other users of the parking community echo Diane's sentiments in grateful feedback messages and testimonials.

Parking Rentals pay *what?*

ParkatmyHouse users in Britain are currently earning as much as $40 per day for short term rentals around stadiums, transportation stations and other busy locations and earn up to **$10,000 a year** for longer term agreements.

Top Do's & Don'ts for Parking Rentals

- Do register with a parking community website such as ParkatmyHouse that allows prospective renters to pull up your available listing for parking on a map of available rentals in the local area. This is the great thing about the Internet; a company can provide the service from afar but help you make connections locally.
- Do provide feedback and accurate ratings once you've consummated a transaction. That's the way the community grows and valid reputations are earned. It helps the integrity of the community when members reward good citizens of the group with favorable ratings and discourage irresponsible participants with truthful criticism.
- Do complete your own profile with the parking matchmaker and connect in your Facebook or other social media profile. More importantly, look for or even request a social media tie-in from prospective renters so that you can feel more comfortable with anyone who will be coming to your property.

- <u>Don't</u> overlook other sources for getting the word out about your available parking space. *Craigslist*, for example, is easy for people to search and has a large, local user base.
- <u>Don't</u> forget to call and check with your homeowner's insurance agent. Let the company know that someone will be parking at your house and make sure that your liability and other coverage is sufficient and up to date. It's good to expect that all will go smoothly but have a plan (and sufficient insurance) in case there are problems.
- <u>Don't</u> be like Medea and risk "parking rage." Next time you're going to an event that you know will have limited parking, check the parking community website. You might be able to arrange a low-cost convenient spot to pull right into when you arrive and avoid all the hassles while keeping a bit more jingle in your pocket!

17. Pick up extra bucks from vehicle storage.

Your home may be a candidate for this storage rental opportunity if you have extra yard space with street or back alley access. Does your home have an accessible side yard? Many RVs will fit in an area that is 10 feet by 20 feet as long as there is sufficient headroom. By the way, you don't necessarily need a concrete pad underneath. Adding some gravel on the ground would be adequate.

What's the advantage of your location?

Wherever you live, your location surely offers a benefit to someone looking to stash an RV, boat or other vehicle. Are you relatively close to an airport—i.e. within 15-20 minutes? You'd be surprised how many people commute by air from one area to another and need to keep a vehicle long term at their destination.

Do you live on a traffic corridor between a metropolitan area and an outlying recreation area? One enterprising homeowner, situated along the route between a major urban area and three recreational lakes, advertised his yard as parking space for a boat or RV at a far lower cost than the going rates in either the city or the resort area. Weekend warriors need only drive out of the city in their cars, stop off and pick up the boat or RV, and continue on to their resort destination. When the fun is done, they drop off the boat or RV on the way back home.

Perhaps your property is relatively close to an attraction—the beach, a tourist destination, or recreation area—but it's not very conveniently located. No problem, simply find an attractive price that will entice a renter to go a few miles out of the way.

It helps to provide a few amenities for your renter in the storage yard such as an air and water station for basic servicing of the vehicle. RV tires can deflate as they sit on the lot, vehicles need water reservoirs refilled, and boats need a quick rinse before long-term storage. Your renter will be impressed that you're providing the kinds of amenities normally found at commercial storage facilities.

Vehicle Storage in Your Yard pays *what?*

Check with one of the major storage chains regarding rates to park or store RVs, boats, and other vehicles so you know what your prospective customers are finding in the marketplace. Also check availability since you can charge more if space is scarce.

Be sure to check local classified listings and look up these rentals on Craigslist.org to discover the going rates from a private party. Remember that as a private party, your price will need to be far enough below commercial rates to attract renters. You can charge more for storing an RV or boat than you would for parking a car since they take up more space. Rates typically are higher during summer months so the best approach is to find renters looking for long-term storage that starts during the summer months.

Top Do's & Don'ts for Vehicle Storage in Your Yard

- Do add a locking gate to an already fenced parking area so you can advertise the space as "Gated and Locked Parking/Storage Available." You'll be able to charge a higher rental rate.
- Do ask for an emergency contact on the application and determine whether someone else will be authorized to access the vehicle. You want to keep *Grand Theft Auto* a computer game only and not anything that actually happens on your property.
- Do clarify that the available space is for parking or storage only, no living on-site! If you were willing to have a tenant move onto your property in an RV, for example, you could provide the hook-ups but it would be at a much higher rate.

- Don't provide continuous hook-ups for water and electricity. If the renter wants to wash down the RV or fill up the water tank, provide a water station or stretch a hose on a temporary basis for that occasional purpose. (See previous pointer.)
- Don't allow vehicles that are unregistered or not road-worthy. You don't want to end up with a junkyard on your property.
- Don't fail to put all terms of the rental agreement in writing including the exact location being rented within your yard (attaching a sketched map is helpful), hours of access, and any rules or limitations.

18. Earn money from storage container rentals.

This rental opportunity suits a home with a large accessible yard that is not necessarily fenced or gated. Since the tenant will lock the storage container that is otherwise impervious to break-ins, he or she does not need to keep the container in a fenced and gated area. You may have to skip this one if you live in a gated community since the homeowner's association probably would not approve keeping a large storage container on your property.

Keep an eye on the freebie section of Craigslist.org in your area for any storage containers that owners are willing to give away just to get them hauled off. The moving fee will set you back a significant sum, but you can charge more for storage if you provide the container.

The Need for Private Storage Containers
One of my real estate clients was so desperate for a place to put his large storage container that he asked me to find a small piece of land that he could *purchase*! He was moving out of California and needed to store equipment and tools for use during occasional trips back to the area to work as an independent contractor for his former employer. He would have been happy to pay a homeowner a significant fee to park his storage container in their yard.

Contractor storage yards charge big bucks to allow customers to house their own storage containers or rent the firm's containers. These commercial firms offer more services and facilities than you would be able to offer in your backyard, but they charge accordingly. One contractors' storage facility that I know of keeps a full-time mechanic onsite to work on their customers' machinery to minimize down time. Their facility provides password-controlled electronic gate access, 24-hour video surveillance, and 10-foot fencing with razor wire around the entire facility.

How can a homeowner compete with those facilities and amenities? Actually, you don't need to compete since companies that need that level of service probably would not rent from you in any case. However, with the rise of foreclosures, the fall of the economy, and the increase in commercial storage rates, many previous or in flux homeowners would be happy to pay you well to store their belongings in a private storage container on your property.

Private Storage Container Rentals pay *what?*

Knowledge is power so, again, check local classified listings and look up these rentals on Craigslist.org to discover the going rates from a private party.

You could charge up to $100 per month or more for a 20-foot container and up to $175 per month or more for a 40-foot container depending on the desirability of your location. Giving renters the flexibility of a month-to-month rental or a long-term lease will also attract more prospective tenants to choose from.

Top Do's & Don'ts for Renting Private Storage Containers

- <u>Do</u> have a written agreement and collect the first month's rent plus a security deposit before you allow anyone to place a large storage container on your property. Realize that you could not easily move or dispose of the container if things were to go badly with the tenant.
- <u>Do</u> run a background check on a prospective renter and require a written application with references. You don't want unsavory folks storing questionable items on your property.
- <u>Do</u> consider the aesthetic impact of having a large container on your property especially if it's visible from the street since rustic containers can be an eyesore. Try to camouflage it behind a tall hedge or plant some fast-growing bamboo to preserve your home's curb appeal. Realize that there could also be a noise problem if your tenant needs frequent access.

- <u>Don't</u> fail to find out how much commercial firms charge in your area so you don't set your fee too low. As a private party you will have to charge far less than a commercial firm, but it's helpful to do the comparison.
- <u>Don't</u> rent to the first person that comes along. This type of storage rental could run for years and you'll have repeated contact with the renter so check out each prospect thoroughly.
- <u>Don't</u> forget to check neighborhood restrictions and local zoning codes. You don't want to have a renter install their storage container and get situated only to discover that it will have to be removed.

Chapter Five. Converting Clutter to Cash

My favorite philosopher George Carlin pointed out that "a house is just a pile of Stuff with a cover on it." Along those lines, a more serious study by UCLA researchers uncovered the fact that 3 out of 4 garages don't house cars because they're too full of bins and boxes of cast-off household goods and discarded furniture.[18]

A team of UCLA researchers examined the material possessions of busy middle-class families and reported the findings in their book entitled *Life at Home in the 21st Century*. They also found that "each new child in a household leads to a 30-percent increase in a family's inventory of possessions during the preschool years alone." So if you have children or have not disposed of your possessions after having raised children, you probably have plenty of clutter that you could convert to cash.

One of the first things you can do to generate cash from your home is sell some of the many belongings that you don't need that have accumulated around your home and in the garage. You can keep your day job while becoming a virtual super salesperson thanks to new technologies that do much of the work for you. You'll benefit not only by raising cash but also by clearing the way for more lucrative uses of your home.

"But I don't have anything to sell," most homeowners would say. Consider this: Nielsen Research and eBay discovered that the average American household has around 50 unused items lying around the house worth about $3,100! If you've been a homeowner for a decade or longer, you probably have 10 to 100 times that amount in accumulated Stuff, with a capital "S", that you wouldn't even miss if you sold it.

The homes that I visit as a real estate agent have far more than 50 unused items lying around. I put the estimate at a minimum of 500 items to over several thousand forgotten but saleable goods. And I'm not referring to candidates for the *Hoarders* TV show! Ordinary people who've lived in their homes for many years tend to collect an enormous amount of Stuff.

I confess I was one of those homeowners who thought I had only a couple dozen items that could be sold on eBay *at the very most*! After enlisting the whole family in the quest for turning clutter into cash, I discovered literally thousands of items that we piled into boxes and shipped off to an online seller. By the way, kids love to get in on the activity if they get a cut of the profit.

Once you ship things off (at an ultra discounted mailing rate *below* book/media rates of the U.S. Postal Service), you sit back and read the emailed reports of your sales and profits. The online seller does everything else: takes the orders, ships the products, and ultimately sends you the cash!

19. Cash in store credits after "reverse shopping."

Shopping, as you know, refers to perusing the items for sale in a store, selecting and paying for your purchases, and bringing the goods home. *Reverse shopping* refers to the opposite process: perusing items in your house or garage that look unused, returning them to a store, and receiving either a cash refund or a store credit that you can sell online for cash.

Need cash fast? This technique can put cash in your pocket within a day or two. Many retail stores will issue a store credit if a returned item looks new, is in the original packaging, and has a tag or UPC on it. (UPC stands for "Universal Product Code," which looks like a small rectangle of skinny black bars that computers use for price scanning at checkout.) The UPC is your friend especially for returns when you have no receipt.

One Homeowner's Clutter-to-Cash Story

At first, Ralph thought he had almost nothing sitting around that he could return to a store. After learning about "reverse shopping," Ralph trolled his garage and managed to collect several very large sacks full of items that looked unused and sported a UPC code: packages of nuts and bolts, unused brushes and paint cans, unopened containers of putty and compound, left-over building materials, plumbing and electrical parts, unopened packages of hardwood floor boards, and much more. He even found some loose boards and other building materials sitting around that had UPC labels on them.

He headed off to the hardware store that he shopped at most often and got in the "returns" line with his sacks and materials piled into a shopping cart. He watched as the clerk scanned each item and was amazed that many of the items were recognized by the computer system based on the UPC code. The register kept track of his growing credit. Although not all items were recognized and credited, he was delighted when his total credit topped $750, which the clerk scanned onto a plastic gift card and handed him.

He then took the remaining items to a hardware store that he shopped at less frequently. He repeated the process and ended up with over $1,000 in store credits for his efforts that day. When he got home, Ralph went online to a gift card site that paid him instantly for the larger gift card since the retailer is popular and its gift cards trade like cash.

Ralph proceeded to repeat the process three more times over the next several weeks. His last trip to the hardware store netted him "only" $150 so he handed off the task to his teenage kids who enjoyed finding returnable items and generating some cash for themselves.

Here's what other homeowners are reverse shopping from their garages: packages of screws and nails, extra packages of incandescent lights that you never plan to use since you switched to fluorescent, rolls of tape, unused work gloves, pieces of pipe and wood with UPCs, packages of cabinet handles and knobs, unused tools, and just about anything else with a code that doesn't look used.

One woman told me that many of the items she returned had sat in her garage literally for *years*. But if the computerized checkout system at the hardware store matches the UPC, you can receive a store credit. What's ironic is that the price you receive may be *more* than you originally paid since hardware prices have gone up over the years.

Converting Store Credits to Cash

Did you know that you could receive cash for your store credits? There are a variety of websites that buy, sell, and trade gift cards for up to 80 to 95 percent of the face value of the gift card.

Say, for example, that you return items to a hardware store that issues you a refund in the form of a merchandise credit worth $100. You could go online the same day and receive $85 or more back on your credit card. Check the companion website *CashCowCasa.com* to discover websites that are currently buying gift cards and merchandise credits. Be aware that any merchandise credit has to be in the form of a plastic card (the size of a credit card) with no expiration date. Paper copies of store credits that have an expiration date can't be cashed in or traded for other gift cards.

In order to get cash right away, you'll need to visit an online gift card site that offers an "instant redemption" option. Generally, these sites enable you to sell your gift card electronically with no mail-in of the card required. You give all the codes over the phone or Internet and then destroy your gift card once you've been paid for it.

If instant redemption is not possible for the type of card you have, then you must mail it in and wait to receive your check. Gift cards from small specialty stores typically take longer to cash in than gift cards from top, popular retailers.

Top Do's and Don'ts of Reverse Shopping

- Do bring an old receipt if you are reverse shopping clothing or personal items from a department store since they will often credit you the price you originally paid even if the purchase exceeds the timeframe of their return policy and the current price of the item is lower than what you paid.
- Do try reverse shopping an item before you sell it online or at a garage sale. You'll receive closer to the original retail price if not full retail. Certain items may be returned for more than you originally paid, such as hardware, if prices have risen. Despite the 10 to 20 percent you'll lose when subsequently converting your store credit to cash, you'll still come out ahead by returning the item for close to its retail price.
- Do try returning discounted or sale items with red tags to a home goods store regardless of how long ago you purchased the items since some of these stores will credit the marked-down items at the price you paid without question, whether or not you have a receipt.

- Don't bring old receipts for hardware items, unless it's within their return policy period since current hardware prices often exceed what you paid previously.
- Don't bother asking for a cash refund unless you have the receipt and are returning the items within the store's return policy period. They could refuse to return the items altogether. Simply ask for a store credit on one of those plastic cards that you can then sell online for cash.
- Don't bring items into a store using another store's sack or bag especially if you don't have a receipt since the clerk could refuse to allow the return. Look around in your cabinets and garage for the correct bags first. Most likely, you'll find plenty of sacks for reverse shopping.

20. Start selling online as an Amazon merchant.

You'll find plenty of books and websites that teach you how to sell your stuff online. However, if you're reading this book, chances are you're looking to generate some fast cash while spending your time elsewhere—like at your workplace. So this section explains how to start as an Amazon seller, which is easier than you might image.

I became an Amazonian some years ago since Amazon seemed to offer the easiest startup to online selling. All online marketplaces are fairly easy once you get the hang of them, but Amazon really lets you hit the ground running.

What Can You Sell on Amazon?

You probably know already that books, tapes, DVDs and other media sell well online. What you may not realize, however, is that you can sell virtually anything online with a few notable exceptions such as medicines, contraband, flammables, and other dangerous or restricted items. All items, however, have to be in "acceptable" condition to be listed on Amazon. If you have broken things that you'd like to sell for scrap or salvage, you can use other online marketplaces such as eBay or Craigslist, but not Amazon.

It's worth 10 minutes to simply browse *Amazon.com* to see the vast array of products available there. Click "Shop by Department" and discover that customers buy everything from grocery items and toys to luggage and pet supplies from Amazon.

Nearly every household has dozens if not hundreds of media items sitting around including books, tapes, DVDs, and CDs. Yet these things represent *old* technology. Today consumers increasingly get their media from iTunes, streaming video, online television and other information stored virtually in the "cloud." If you need cash now, it makes sense to sell most of your physical media while there are still plenty of buyers for that old technology. Special editions and collectables are the exception, of course, since digital cloud storage won't replace them.

Realize that you only can offer products that already have an existing listing on Amazon. Your merchandise "piggy backs" on a listing that other merchants have established. Since the listing already exists, you don't have to take digital photos, enter product descriptions, or write marketing copy. You simply add a few words about your item's condition and set the price you want. Someone else has already done the heavy lifting of writing the complete product description and uploading product photos.

If you do want to sell unique or one-of-a-kind items that are not already posted for sale on Amazon, then you'll need to pay for the enhanced service that allows you to enter new listings into Amazon's database of products. Pro Merchant, for example, is a subscription service that makes sense for sellers who sell more than several dozen items a month. The service allows you to create new listings and provides other benefits while reducing the per-item fees that Amazon normally charges when an item sells.

Amazon as Your Shipping & Customer Service Dept.

The easiest way to sell on Amazon is to use their "fulfillment" services. With Fulfillment by Amazon (FBA), you store your gear in Amazon's fulfillment centers. The company takes orders for your stuff from customers and then packs, ships, and provides customer service for your items.

Once you enter each item into the Amazon system, you put it all in a large box and mail it to an Amazon fulfillment center. The company takes it from there. Amazon employees unpack the box and store your merchandise, take orders 24/7, collect payment, ship the product out to the consumer, deduct service fees, and send you a payment. It's like handing the process off to your own shipping and customer service departments.

It will take you 10 minutes or so to register as an Amazon seller. Begin by typing in the title or UPC of a book or other item you'd like to sell. Once the preexisting listing for the item displays, look on the right side for the question "Have one to sell?" Next to that question is a link labeled "Sell on Amazon." Clicking the link allows you to list your item if you're already an Amazon seller or sign up if it's your first time trying to sell something on Amazon.

Once you click to list an item, you'll have to select a category for its condition (i.e. *New, Used Like New, Very Good, Good* etc.) and type in a few details about its condition. For example, a book in *Good* condition might be further explained as, "Dust jacket missing, clean pages, creases on spine." A CD in *Good* condition could be further described as, "Scratches on CD that don't affect playback, includes all inserts." After entering the quantity you have to sell (usually "1") and the price desired, you're done.

Pricing is fairly quick and easy to do. The system generally shows you the lowest price currently offered by other Amazon sellers as well as the full retail or list price. If you're motivated to have a fast sale, price your merchandise a penny lower than the lowest priced offering of the same quality. Then your product will appear first in the list when buyers search for that product.

Other things being equal, products fulfilled by Amazon display at the top of the search results with a boxed message stating "Fulfillment by Amazon." Buyers can feel more confident in purchasing from FBA sellers since that status lets buyers know that Amazon will ship their order in a timely and careful manner.

Another advantage of using Amazon to fulfill your orders is that there is no shipping charge added to the price of your merchandise. Therefore, if the lowest priced book from a non-FBA seller was $4.00 plus a shipping charge of $3.99, for example, you as an FBA seller could charge $7.50 and still save the buyer money.

The system will display your $7.50 item as being less expensive than the $4.00 item since Amazon considers the *total* price, including shipping, when displaying items from least to most expensive in search results.

There are no upfront fees to list merchandise on Amazon unless you sign up for special privileges. Amazon does have small fees to store, sell, and ship your products, and the company deducts these fees from the proceeds at the time of sale. If you sell books, music, or videos, you can even make your products eligible for international sales. Your products will be marketed to millions (soon to be billions!) of prospective buyers and you'll have world-class customer service and shipping departments behind you.

Top Do's & Don'ts of Selling on Amazon

- <u>Do</u> use Amazon's fulfillment service FBA (Fulfillment by Amazon) if you have lots of things to sell but don't want to handle shipping each item separately. For a modest fee, they take care of all orders and shipping (once you ship your box of stuff to them) so you don't have to turn into an order taker and shipping department. Stick with your day job and let Amazon handle the selling and shipping that they do so very well.

- <u>Do</u> list items that you will ship yourself (i.e. "Merchant fulfillment") if you are in a big hurry to sell. As an FBA merchant, realize that your products won't go "live" on the Amazon system until after your FBA shipment box is received at an Amazon fulfillment center. If you are fulfilling an order yourself, your listing appears on Amazon as soon as you enter it. So you could list something in the morning, receive an order, and ship it out in the afternoon.

- <u>Do</u> review your inventory periodically to make sure your pricing remains competitive. Ever wondered why Amazon merchandise often has unusual pricing such as *$19.73*? It's probably because the seller dropped the price a penny below the next lowest offer to capture the coveted top-of-list position in search results.

- <u>Don't</u> list anything that you absolutely would not want returned for a refund especially if you use Fulfillment by Amazon. No seller wants returns, but expensive items that could be returned within 90 days pose a special problem for small sellers who may have spent the proceeds of a sale already. Unless Amazon changes its liberal return and refund policies, you may want to sell expensive items through other online marketplaces.

- <u>Don't</u> waste too much time wading through the online new seller Q&A and help screens. A great benefit for Amazon sellers is that you can pick up the phone and call Amazon support directly. It's helpful to have a live rep walk you through the process.

- <u>Don't</u> use Amazon's fulfillment service to sell brand new software, CDs, or DVDs still in unopened boxes since Amazon will issue 100 percent refunds for any returns. Buyers could open and return the products for a full refund without a restocking fee deducted. Then you'd have to lower the price and sell the return as a used item. It's better to sell these unopened items directly as an Amazon merchant so you can charge a restocking fee or sell them through a different channel such as eBay where you can bar returns altogether.

21. Sell virtually anything on eBay.

While Amazon makes it very easy to hit the ground running as an online seller by allowing you to piggyback your products onto established listings, eBay has gone a step further for common products by providing canned product descriptions and stock photos. Typically, however, to list your gear on eBay, you'll need to write your own product descriptions and upload digital photos that you've taken yourself or found elsewhere on the web.

You can list virtually anything on eBay: an air cleaner or lamp, a fraternity pin or other jewelry, spare car parts, clothing, antiques, collectibles, sporting goods, box tops and reward points, junked electronics sold as "scrap"—you name it. It may seem like trash to you, but it may be just the thing that someone else has been searching for everywhere.

You can sell things on eBay that are not in working condition. In contrast, Amazon requires all listings to be in "Acceptable" working condition at a minimum. On eBay, you select from a variety of categories such as "New," "Used," "Manufacturer refurbished," or "For parts or not working." The latter description applies to items that don't work, possess various defects, or have missing parts. You'd be surprised how many people will pay money for those junked items piled in your closet or garage!

Too Busy? Use an eBay Trading Assistant

If you don't have time for online sales, consider using a "trading assistant." Unlike Amazon, eBay offers a cadre of trading assistants to take care of the sales process for you. Some of these assistants operate a physical storefront with regular business hours.

Similar to a consignment store, eBay stores take your dropped-off items, or even offer a pick-up service, and pay you the proceeds of your eBay sales less their fees and commissions. You'll make about a third less but you get to skip the hassles of researching and pricing your stuff, snapping and uploading digital photos, listing, negotiating, and shipping. If your day job keeps you too busy to dabble in online sales, this solution helps you convert your home's clutter to cash with minimal time on your part. To learn more, go to the Selling menu at *eBay.com* and choose "Sell it for me."

Know Your Stuff

An important aspect of selling an item for top dollar is to know what you have and what it's worth. If you use an eBay trading assistant, that person will know how to price your item for maximum return in the shortest amount of time.

It helps to know the range of prices already being asked for the item and, like Amazon, eBay reveals the lowest price for an identical item in a similar condition. For example, if you are listing a used DVD, eBay will show you the lowest price on the system for that particular DVD in used condition. Then you can decide if you want to go below that price to score a quick sale or price it higher and wait.

It helps to turn into a sleuth. Grab a magnifying glass to search for brand names, model numbers, and other markings on your belongings that have no UPC. Check the website of the manufacturer or designer for more info on your merchandise. You also may find an image there to use in your listing. Knowledge is power.

For most of your items, Google will be your best ally in figuring out what you have and what it's worth. Simply type a description of the item into Google's search engine for a broader view of how much others are asking across the web, not just on eBay. In many cases, you may discover that your things are worth *more* than you expected.

Score Power

After every eBay transaction, the buyer and seller rate one another and those ratings form the basis of your reputation on eBay. The key to successful selling on eBay lies in building a good reputation so buyers will be comfortable doing business with you. Unlike Amazon where the company stands behind every sale with their "A to Z" guarantee that refunds a purchase for any reason, eBay requires buyers to rely on your prior track record in deciding whether or not to do business with you. There also are some newer initiatives that give buyers more protection from unscrupulous sellers.

There are the obvious ways to achieve high seller scores and a few lesser-known approaches. Of course, you'll want to respond quickly to buyer inquires, describe items accurately, and ship promptly. However, being a good seller is only part of the story. You'll need to protect yourself from "bad" buyers. Think of it as defensive driving on the online superhighway.

Protecting Your Seller Ratings from "Bad" Buyers

The eBay system allows you to protect yourself by blocking certain types of buyers. That way, they won't cause problems and then turn around and issue *you* negative feedback like the problem was your fault. Brand new buyers on eBay, for example, may have unreasonable expectations, or they may be buyers with a bad reputation who've dumped a tarnished eBay identity for a brand new one with a clean slate. If you're a new seller who has not yet established a solid reputation, you're better off avoiding first-time buyers. Here are other buyers you may wish to avoid:

- Anyone who does not have a PayPal account. Holders of an account must verify their address and identity so it gives you more assurances that you're dealing with someone who has been "checked out."
- Buyers who have received "unpaid item strikes," which means they won an auction or clicked to buy an item but never paid for it.
- Buyers with reported violations or a negative feedback score.

There are presets you can select to block these undesirable buyers and it makes good sense to do so. Don't worry that you'll lose business. There are millions of prospects on eBay and you don't need to expose yourself to potential problems and negative feedback unnecessarily, especially when you're first trying to get your good reputation established.

eBay Sales pay *what?*

It's not hard to hit the ground running with **hundreds of dollars in sales every day**. There are a few catches, however.

First, it takes time to set up your eBay account along with a connected PayPal account as you are verified and your bank account linked.

Second, PayPal most likely will restrict your account and not release funds for 21 days or 3 days after delivery confirmation, whichever comes first. After meeting certain criteria, your account restrictions are lifted and you have instant access to your cash via your PayPal debit card although there may be a daily cash withdrawal limit.

Top Do's & Don'ts of eBay Selling

- Do take well-lit digital pictures and include several from different angles so prospective buyers feel assured about the item's condition. It helps to photograph an item against a plain background so that attention is focused on the product not the surroundings.
- Do describe your item accurately and price it competitively. Balance your snappy marketing copy with an honest statement of the flaws. Then deliver exactly what you advertise. Otherwise, expect complaints and poor ratings. Also check out how much others are charging so your pricing is not out of line. It doesn't matter what you paid when you purchased the item, pricing depends only on the current market value.
- Do add tracking to every shipment and take advantage of discounted online postage rates. One click lets you print a shipping label with pre-paid postage charged instantly to your PayPal account. Besides getting a discount on postage, you won't have to waste time standing in line at the post office.

- Don't forget about your own safety. When allowing buyers to come pick up an item, be careful. If a buyer comes to your home for "local pickup," make sure someone else is there with you.
- Don't do business with "bad buyers" who have violations, negative feedback scores, and other strikes against them. The eBay system lets sellers block sales to these types of buyers, and new sellers should take advantage of this feature.
- Don't underestimate the time that online sales will take between getting the item listed in the first place, dealing with prospective customers, and shipping the product out. You might be better off using one of eBay's approved trading assistants to handle the whole process for you.

22. Connect with local buyers through Craigslist.

Craigslist (at *Craigslist.org*) is a mostly free, local-oriented posting service that allows you to list items that can be searched daily by prospective buyers. An increasingly popular service in over 700 localities, Craigslist users post over 50 million new classified listings every month and generate 30 billion page views a month! Postings are ordered according to the date entered with the most recently posted item displayed first. There are dozens of categories ranging from *Appliances, Antiques, Bikes* and *Boats* to *Music, Photos, Toys, Videogames* and so much more. A posting consists of a brief description of the item and up to four photos.

Craigslist works surprisingly well because it's both local and timely. It lacks the built-in controls and safeguards you'll find on eBay and Amazon since no money is being collected or exchanged by the service. You'll have to exercise your own judgment when deciding whether or not to meet a prospective buyer or have them come to your home.

Exercise Caution

Everything is completely anonymous unless you include your phone number in the posting. Otherwise, a prospective buyer will email you via the system that will forward the message to your personal email. Once you arrange a meeting either by phone or email with the buyer, money and goods are exchanged when buyer and seller meet face-to-face.

Despite the notorious stories of Craigslist crimes, everyone I know using Craigslist—and that includes my own family—has had nothing but good experiences. It's a better, faster, and cheaper way to attract local buyers than advertising in your local newspaper or penny shopper. Be sure to talk with a prospective buyer before arranging a meeting. Then listen to your inner voice. If the buyer seems weird or spooky, of course, you wouldn't give out your home address or arrange a meeting. When arranging any meeting at your home, make sure someone else is there with you.

You do have to watch out for scams on Craigslist. A scam generally starts out with a generic rather than specific response to your post. A popular one goes like this: "I am willing to make a deal ASAP. Your response will be appreciated." Notice that the message says nothing about your particular item and could apply to any product or service.

A genuine response to a Craigslist ad for a camera might read something like this: "I'm interested in your Sony camera and wonder if it comes with an extra battery, lens, and case." Real responses from real prospective buyers are not vague and general. They pose specific questions about the item.

The Upside of Craigslist

Anybody can jump right in and start making money with Craigslist. There's virtually no setup or wait time like you'll encounter before receiving cash from Amazon and eBay sales. Since there is no exchange of money on Craigslist, you don't have to link your bank account, as Amazon requires, or set up a PayPal account, as eBay prompts you to do.

The best thing about Craigslist is that you can list your item in the morning and pocket cash by the afternoon. There are no restrictions or payment holds like those imposed by the other online selling sites. You don't have to hassle with packing or shipping. You do have to exercise good judgment in arranging a meeting with the prospective buyer since sales occur face-to-face.

Craigslist Sales pay *what?*

For heavy, big-ticket items such as furniture and appliances, Craigslist is hard to beat. While you could list these items for "local pickup only" on a national forum such as eBay, there's no need to give up a significant percentage of the sale, sometimes up to 20 percent, between the online marketplace and the payment processor when Craigslist enables you to connect with the buyer and transact a cash sale directly.

Craigslist allows you to keep 100 percent of the proceeds of the sale. Sell your piano listed on Craigslist for $2,000, for instance, and pocket $2000. Sell it through eBay, and you'll be paying eBay over $80 and PayPal nearly $60. By the way, eBay has acquired a significant stake in Craigslist more recently by purchasing its stock.

Top Do's & Don'ts for Selling on Craigslist

- Do deal locally with people you can meet in person if you're going to transact business using Craigslist. If you stick with face-to-face transactions, you will avoid 99 percent of the scams that you may have heard about being perpetrated through Craigslist.
- Do take good digital photos and keep your photos organized and easily accessible from your hard drive, because you may have to upload them multiple times. Since your listing expires and needs to be relisted each week, the text and headline can be relisted with one click but photos may not be saved and must be re-uploaded unless you use special software that automates the process.
- Do repost your ad often if you're highly motivated to sell your stuff. Buyers read the most recently posted items first and may not look past postings that are more than a day or two old. If you repost before the ad expires, the photos are included and don't have to uploaded separately.

- Don't post your phone number numerically. If you decide to include your number, use a combination of words and numbers so a machine can't extract the number. For example, type something like "555-one two 12" instead of "555-1212."

- Don't believe email responses at face value, be discerning. Notice whether the response is generic rather than specific to the item you posted. Be especially wary of a request to mail the item or pay via PayPal since the transaction could be reversed. For example, ignore emails that say, "I'm interested in your item but can't pick it up so please mail and I'll pay with PayPal."
- Don't expect Craigslist to bail you out if you fall for a scam. The company does not handle payments or guarantee transactions, as does Amazon. Again, be very observant of what a prospect says and does not say. Be wary if the prospective buyer gives excuses as to why he or she can't come pay cash and pick up the merchandise directly. Requests for shipping or for the use of PayPal probably mean that it's a scam.

23. Recycle and "scrap" for cash.

This section is not about standing in line at the local collection center for plastic bottles and aluminum cans--although that experience may get you in touch with some rather interesting people in America. However, you'd be surprised how much money you can generate from other types of scrapping and recycling while clearing out your home for some of the more profitable endeavors described in this book.

Cash for Your Used Technology

Technology cast-offs make good candidates for recycling. There are a number of companies, mostly online, that pay good money for your used technology gear. With a few clicks, you can tell them what you have, get a bid for what they'll pay you (IF you describe it accurately), and print a label for free mailing to the recycler. Check the companion website for this book *CashCowCasa.com* for recyclers that pay cash for used technology.

Other candidates for recycling include used ink cartridges, printers, and cell phones. Some brands of used cartridges bring as much as $3.50 to $4.00 *each*. That may not sound like much, but you'd be surprised just how many of those little buggers you've probably got lying around.

A few years ago before going mostly paperless (*Will I ever go truly paperless?*), I went on a cartridge hunt one afternoon and found an old garbage bag full of used cartridges in my garage! As I kept looking, I found dozens more in drawers and cabinets, several bags full of empty ones stashed in my home office, a bunch of unopened ones that had expired in the office supply closet, a few still inside junked printers, and a big sack of used cartridges in my car trunk waiting to be donated.

After checking online, I found a list of companies that buy used cartridges including one with an office nearby. So I took my cartridge collection to them directly rather than mailing and received a check for over $700. Not bad for devoting a couple hours to clearing out some clutter.

Many of the same recycling companies that buy cartridges pay for old printers, computers, and even your old cell phones. If your home is like many households, you probably have a few printers and old computers piled up in your garage or closets, a drawer full of dead cell phones, and a bag of assorted TV remotes, right? You can sell this gear online if it's newer and unbroken. The older items or broken gear can be sold for scrap via Craigslist or eBay or simply sold (or donated) to a recycler.

Urban Mining

Did you know that a growing percentage of certain metals and materials now come through the process of "urban mining," which refers to recycling materials such as aluminum, steel, copper, and even gold and silver! Scrap metal prices are near all-time highs driven by high worldwide demand and dwindling supply.

Many homeowners may not realize it, but they have a significant amount of metal scrap sitting around the house right now. Take gold for example. As the price of gold goes up, it becomes economic to mine your home for gold scrap. Virtually every electronic device and connector has gold scrap in it—every computer, cell phone, phone plug, cable box… you name it. While it's a complicated process to extract the gold through a refining process, a homeowner can sell items containing gold scrap to a scrapper who amasses tons of scrap and then sells it in bulk to a refiner.

By the way, that authoritative website on all subjects, *Jokes4us.com* answers the age-old question:
"Q: Why is there no gold at the end of the rainbow?
 A: The Leprachan took it and sold it to Cash4Gold!"

It might be worth it to you to check your jewelry boxes and drawers for scrap jewelry. Over the years, you may have thrown an odd earring in a drawer when the matching one was lost, set aside the extra gold links from a watch you had resized, or forgot about that gold bracelet that got bent and tossed aside. With gold at all time highs, you may be quite surprised how much those odds and ends will fetch from a gold buyer. You can look for a local buyer of scrap gold or turn to one of the online gold buying companies. They generally provide the mailing container that tracks and insures your gold shipment to them, which they assess and then send you a check.

As a sign of the times, you may have to get clearance from local authorities before selling copper scrap. Too many enterprising thugs have stripped vacant homes and foreclosures of their copper pipe to sell for scrap. So now even legitimate homeowners who want to clear out some old copper pipe lying on the garage floor may need to get permission before selling it to a scrapper.

Top Do's & Don'ts of Recycling

- Do business with reputable online firms that let you track any shipment of recycled items that you sell to them. Trying to find a local scrapper can be time-consuming and prove unproductive once you do find them. There are many reputable firms on the Internet today that you can trust. Look for the various third party endorsements and designations on their site to ease any concerns you may have.
- Do expect your recycler to provide free mailers or pre-printed shipping labels. Then all you have to do is pack the recyclables in a box, affix the label, and drop off the box at the shipping carrier. Generally, you can ship up to 40 pounds of recyclables for free.
- Do share your newfound knowledge about recycling with your local school or non-profit group so they too can earn extra cash by recycling technology and ink cartridges. Your efforts could help keep tons of solid waste out of landfills and earn your non-profit group extra money.

- Don't recycle late model cell phones unless they're broken. You're better off selling those on eBay or Amazon if they're in working condition since you'll make up to 10 times more.
- Don't give away old laptops and other computers until you first check to see who would pay for them. The CPU and other components on the motherboard generally contain gold. You are literally *giving away gold* when you discard an old computer. Instead, sell to a scrapper who knows how to mine the computer for gold and will pay you for the opportunity.
- Don't throw away or give away scrap metal. You'd be surprised at the resale value of common metals such as steel, copper, aluminum, stainless steel and others. Collect metal items as you clean out your garage and sell to a local metal scrapper. You can find their ads on your local Craigslist.

24. Unlock cash fast with a yard or garage sale.

A garage sale is a great way to connect with your local community, sell some Stuff, pocket a little cash, and maybe even learn a few lessons in human behavior. The prices at a yard sale are typically low, lower, and lowest, but the conversations can be priceless. Take, for example, the *Treasure Hunter* who invariably will show up at your sale:

"I heard that some woman bought a painting at a garage sale that turned out to be worth over a million dollars."

"Oh, really!" you reply.

"Have any paintings like that you wanna sell?"

Then there's the *Bargain Hunter* who asks what you want for your 2-foot tall Roman statue with a chip on the left foot. "Twenty bucks," you answer.

"Last week I saw it new at WalMart for $15," the Hunter retorts.

"Ok, I'll sell it to you for 12."

"I'll give you a buck."

"Sold!"

Yard sales can be far more entertaining than online transactions at eBay or Amazon. It's true that online marketplaces expose your goods to a regional, national, or even worldwide audience of prospective buyers, but the "cash-and-carry" aspect of a yard sale is hard to beat. You can decide on a Friday night to hold a sale, spend your Saturday morning haggling under the hot sun, and by the afternoon enjoy watching a flock of helpers carry off your junk while you count your jingle and celebrate the shipping hassles you've avoided.

    Yard sales offer the advantage of better visibility than *garage* sales although if you've ever held a garage sale, you know the benefit of keeping the garage door closed until you're ready to start the sale. No sale would be complete without the *Early Bird* knocking on your front door at 6 a.m. unless you post "No Early Birds" signs on the garage door or gate (if your property is fenced and securely gated). If you start in the garage, you later can pull unsold items into the yard for better visibility by those who pass by as the sale progresses.

In my role as a real estate agent, I not only enjoy going to garage sales but also have reaped big benefits from holding my own garage sales because of the great connections I've made. The real estate business is inherently local so meeting people from the local area generally leads to business sooner or later.

Hot Tip: If you have some leftover junk that those charity pickup trucks won't even touch, here's a trick that worked for me. Instead of leaving the unsold items at the curb with a sign saying "Free, Help Yourself," mark the box "$5 Each." (You can thank me when everything is gone the next day.)

Derive Benefits by Charging Others

You probably wouldn't want to do this just for the modest amount of cash you'd receive for use of your yard, but the spin-offs can be quite valuable.

Now that you're an expert on holding a yard sale, word will get around and apartment dwellers near and far will pay you big bucks to let them use your yard to make a few dollars for themselves. Ok, not really, but you could run a free ad in Craigslist to offer your facility to yard-less/garage-less folks who would be willing to pay you a modest sum to hold their own yard sale in your yard. As part of the deal, you can ask them to allow you to display an "item" or two.

Watch and Learn. Since you don't have to run around selling your own Stuff for pennies on the dollar, you'll have the chance to sit back and learn a little more about human behavior. Watch all the big fancy cars that stop by the sale. Really, I'm not kidding! The drivers probably spent 10 bucks in gas to get there, which explains why they have to negotiate so vehemently to get that china bowl for $3 instead of $5.

By the way, take a good look at the Stuff on sale. You just might see some of your old junk that got hauled off after your own yard sale, now back for another go-around. It makes you wonder if there's some company that rents out this Stuff week after week to families holding garage sales. (Hey, that could be another strategy for the next edition of *Cash Cow Casa*!)

Incidentally, according to *Reader's Digest*, there are 10 things people should never buy at a rummage sale, mostly for health and safety reasons. They include: helmets, car seats, tires, wetsuits and swim suits, mattresses, cribs, laptops, plasma TVs, shoes, and hats. Oops, I've sold items in every one of these categories over the years either at rummage sales or over the Internet. *Sorry*.

Best of Both Worlds. Getting paid to host someone else's yard sale gives you the best of both worlds. You still get to meet and greet your neighbors and work the crowd for valuable business connections if you choose, but you're free of the hassles and pressures associated with preparing for the sale and having spirited negotiations over chump change.

Best of all, it gives you an opportunity to showcase a couple of high-end item such as a car you'd like to sell. Garage sales are one of the best places to get the word out about your used car, special collectable item, piece of furniture, antique, or *tchotchke*. Many people coming to the sale will know at least one person looking for a used car, for example. Just being on display at the garage sale gives the car or other item an aura of being a great deal.

Chapter Six. Ads, Tower Leases, & Referrals

For maximum cash with minimum hassle, the passive income opportunities in this chapter have the potential to squeeze plenty of cash from your property while you invest your time and energies elsewhere.

Making your house a *cash cow casa* means considering every possible source of cash that you could squeeze from your yard to your rooftop to your property's title.

25. Collect lots of easy cash for tower leases.

Obtaining a lease for a satellite or cell tower is one of the most lucrative ways to put your house to work for you with little time or trouble on your part. Once the tower is installed, you can sit back and collect your monthly checks, generally for many years. As mobile computing and smart phones proliferate, the need for more towers is growing fast.

Your local planning or zoning office can tell you what the requirements are for installing a cell or satellite tower and whether or not your property can meet those requirements. If your home is a tower candidate, you could join the hundreds of thousands of properties nationwide that host cell sites.

It's important to differentiate between cell phone carriers and tower companies. The cell phone carriers are companies such as Verizon, AT&T, T-Mobile, Sprint and various other companies operating a cell phone network. A tower company is in the business of leasing from the property owner and then subleasing to one or more phone companies. The distinction is important since in one case you would be dealing directly with the paying company and in the other case you would be dealing with a middleman.

When dealing with a middleman (i.e. the tower company), you face more risk since a new lease could be terminated before you ever collect rent. The reason is that the tower company is *speculating* that they can sublease to at least one or more cell phone carriers. If the expected subleasing does not materialize, the tower company might cancel the deal with you.

Are you a candidate?
Your property may or may not qualify as a candidate for a cell tower. Some experts have estimated that the average homeowner has less than a five percent chance of obtaining a lucrative cell tower

lease.[19] Wireless carriers generally pinpoint specific geographic sites for locating their towers based on very specific radio frequency engineering standards and economic models of anticipated business activity. Based on the results, these wireless carriers often approach cell tower candidates rather than the property owner approaching the companies.

My philosophy, learned the hard way, is to reach out for a cell tower lease before it goes to someone else. Some years ago, I was thinking about contacting a satellite Internet provider since there was no broadband service available in the mountainous area where I lived at the time. Unfortunately, I procrastinated while my next-door neighbor contacted a provider and ended up getting a lucrative tower lease on his property.

There are certain factors that do make your property more or less likely as a cell tower candidate. If you might be a candidate, there are some things you can do to try to capture this opportunity.

Here are some factors that may make your property more or less likely to be leased.[20] A cell tower lease is:

- More likely if you are not within a mile of another tower. Besides the fact that the carrier would not want to duplicate coverage, the local zoning jurisdiction will require use of existing towers first.
- More likely if you are in an urban or suburban area or near a high-traffic roadway.
- More likely if you have favorable zoning that allows a tower to be placed on your property.
- More likely if you have a roof capable of handling a minimum of 150 pounds per square foot of roof loading in an area of at least 20 feet by 30 feet.

- Less likely if you live on farmland surrounded by other farmland unless you live within a ¼ mile of a major highway or 4-lane road.
- Less likely if you have a pitched roof rather than a flat roof.
- Less likely if you cannot provide or are unwilling to provide 24-hour access, 7 days a week, 365 days a year to all portions of the tower facility.

Reach Out and Touch… a Carrier
Be sure to check with local zoning authorities before you bother contacting cell carriers and tower companies since it would be a waste of time if your zoning does not allow communication structures.

Assuming that your property does qualify as "more likely" to host a cell site, the next step is to contact the carriers and tower companies if you don't want to wait for them to contact you. Many of them allow you to submit your property online for consideration.

It takes only a few minutes to fill in their online forms. It helps if you know the approximate dimensions of your lot, your GPS coordinates, and height of your home although you can still register your property without that information. Refer to this book's companion website at *CashCowCasa.com* to find links to the submission forms.

Don't expect any response once you register your house with the various carriers and tower companies. Your home gets entered into their databases and you'll be contacted if your property fits what they need. One expert in negotiating cell tower leases recommends that you re-submit your property at least once every few months.

Get Even More Cash from a Lease Buyout

If you are lucky enough to obtain a long-term cell tower lease, then the fun really begins! Some companies will pay you cash for the rights to your lease, referred to as a "buyout" of your lease. The buyout company pays you a one-time lump-sum payment upfront in exchange for the assignment of future rent payments. In exchange for the lump sum, you grant the buyout company an exclusive easement over your property along with the assignment of future rents.

You'll be tempted to grab the money and run, but it's advisable to seek the advice of an appropriate attorney and other professionals before consenting to a buyout. For one thing, when you sell the revenue stream to a lease buyout company, you are not necessarily selling all of your obligations and responsibilities under the original lease. You need to understand if you're still on the hook and for how much.

Another reason to seek professional assistance is that you'll need help in determining the true value of the buyout. According to one expert law firm, most property owners mistakenly "sell out" for well below market value.

Cell Tower Leases pay *what?*

Cell tower lease experts report many leases in the range of **$900 to $1,500** per month and some up to $3,000 a month depending on supply and demand as well as other factors.[21] The typical lease term is 25 years and includes provisions for yearly increases.

If you do snag a contract with a carrier, it's important to know that most wireless carriers pay their sales people a bonus for negotiating company-favorable terms with the homeowner (i.e.

you!). If the sales person can trim the annual rent increase 1%, it could amount to a difference of $170,000 over the life of the lease in favor of the company (and loss to the homeowner).[22] So it literally pays to get expert help.

Top Do's & Don'ts for Satellite and Cell Tower Leases

- <u>Do</u> consult an attorney, consultant, or both who are experienced in negotiating this type of lease. The cost of hiring qualified experts is minimal compared with the money you stand to receive (or lose) over the term of the lease.
- <u>Do</u> check with local permitting authorities first to make sure you can have communications equipment on your property. If you do get a lease, call your insurance agent to determine what additional coverage you may need to add.
- <u>Do</u> take the few minutes needed to fill out the online forms of the major cell carriers and tower companies. The potential cash flow is phenomenal if your property happens to be selected. One expert recommends submitting your property every couple months.

- <u>Don't</u> completely ignore the potential risk to you and your family of having a tower on your property. Although there is no scientific proof of potential harm from RF (radio frequency) exposure, it doesn't hurt to check with a qualified consultant on electromagnetic pollution. Experts claim that having a tower on your roof is the safest since the antennas are directional and send signals outward, not downward.
- <u>Don't</u> assume a carrier will want to install a tower simply due to the fact that there is currently no cell phone coverage in your area for that carrier. Carriers may choose not to cover areas that don't meet certain business criteria.
- <u>Don't</u> waste your money on property listing or management services for cell tower leases. These service groups cannot cover every local market. You, rather than a third party, probably are the best person to market your property to the carriers.

26. Let advertisers pay you to display their ads.

According to the Outdoor Advertising Association of America, advertisers spent nearly $6.4 billion on outdoor advertising last year.[23] Wouldn't you love to have just a tiny fraction of those earnings flow to you! It's unlikely you could place one of those huge 14 ft by 48 ft behemoths in your yard, but there are many smaller signs that might work for your property.

Then again, there are many restrictions on billboards and other signage. Large billboards are banned entirely in several states and many municipalities and other entities restrict or ban signage.

So you have to check with your local authorities. Generally, billboards and other signs only can be placed in commercial, industrial, and agricultural zones.

If you live along a busy street or your home is visible from a street with a fair amount of traffic (either vehicular or pedestrian), you still might be able to make money from advertisers who want to get out their message in your area. Even if you live in a strictly residential area with a small yard, your *home* itself could become a billboard as you'll find out below.

Is Your Property a Candidate for a Billboard?
If you think your property might be well located for outdoor advertising, you'll first need to check several factors before calling a billboard company. According to one billboard expert, knowing whether or not you're a candidate for a billboard will depend on your answers to the following questions.[24]

Good visibility? Would a sign have sufficient visibility from the street to allow viewers to spend 4 to 5 seconds reading the sign?
Good Traffic? It's helpful to know the amount of traffic that travels your street. Just as Internet ads pay based on the amount of "traffic" or users that come to a site, billboards pay according to the amount of traffic that passes by the prospective billboard.
Appropriate Zoning? Look up your property profile online or check with your local planning and zoning department to find out your property's zoning classification. Then inquire about the permissibility of signs and billboards on properties with that zoning. In general, if your property is zoned "agricultural," it may qualify if it's not on a road that receives federal funding.

If your zoning is strictly residential, then your property may not qualify unless you can get the zoning changed. I live in an area where most of the single-family homes are on land zoned "light agricultural."
Government regulation? The Highway Beautification Act of the mid 1960's established restrictions on outdoor advertising. Large billboards were restricted to commercial or industrial areas broadly defined. You can check on your local and state laws that govern billboards by calling your local planning and building department. Or if you home is located along a state- or federally-funded highway, then you'll need to contact your state's department of transportation and talk with the people in the outdoor advertising division.

<u>Adequate sign separation?</u> The Beautification Act also regulates the spacing between signs as well as size and other aspects. In addition, most cities have their own ordinances on signs that add yet another layer of regulation and specification on signage. It's a job to learn all these rules so it's a good idea to use a professional who knows the rules and how to work around them in your area.

Making Your *Home* the Billboard

This one is either a cool, novel idea or the reason that homeowners associations and zoning restrictions can be a good thing. Have you ever seen one of those cars painted ("wrapped") with an ad for some product or service? Now you can turn your home into an urban or suburban billboard by a company that pays your mortgage while they display an ad on your home.[25] They claim they'll paint your home's exterior from top to bottom to create the ad then paint it back to the original colors when the ad contract expires.

Naysayers to this idea point out that good neighbors wouldn't paint an ad on their home because it could hurt property values. Proponents of the idea point out that having an ad for three months, if it helps a neighbor stave off foreclosure, might be less harmful to property values than the alternative—foreclosure and a house sitting vacant in the neighborhood.

This idea could make sense for you if your home is not in a homeowners association and as long as local zoning ordinances don't prohibit it. The idea here is novel but the jury is still out on this one. The company has received tens of thousands of applications from homeowners but results are slow in forthcoming. I say, "Don't hold your breath on this one, but still, it's worth the few seconds it will take you to fill out the application." Check our website at *CashCowCasa.com* for the current link.

Billboards pay *what?*

If your property is zoned "agricultural" and you succeed in renting billboard space to a billboard company, you could receive monthly lease payments, a lump sum cash payment, or a combination of the two. Billboard revenue spans a wide range since it's based on many factors, primarily traffic counts. Actually what you're renting out is a "ground lease" to a sign company that, in turn, rents the display space to advertisers.

The rent you receive typically is a percentage of the amount of ad revenue generated by the sign. The percentage varies from 10 percent to 20 percent of the ad revenue. For example, if the billboard makes about $4,000 per month in ad revenue, first you would assume a 70 percent occupancy rate since the billboard will not be used 100 percent of the time (depending on its location). Ten percent of the total revenue, adjusted for the vacancy rate, would yield you $280 per month. That rent is cash flow that requires no hassle with tenants and essentially no effort on your part whatsoever once it's set up.

For homes zoned "residential," your only option may be to turn to the house "wrap" ad scheme that pays your mortgage payment each month while the ad remains painted onto your home's exterior. Hey, you just might end up getting your house repainted for free.

Top Do's & Don'ts for Billboard Rentals

- Do your homework and gather data about zoning restrictions, local rates that others are making on billboards, size of billboard structures, traffic counts on your street and so on.
- Do consult an attorney, consultant, or both who are experienced in negotiating sign and billboard leases in your area. Share the data you've gathered.
- Do check (or have your attorney/consultant check) with local permitting authorities to make sure your signage conforms to applicable local and state laws.

- Don't assume that you will have a say over the content displayed on the billboard. Typically you only can restrict "objectionable" content.
- Don't ignore the downside of billboards: the noise, lighting, and liability. Who will pay if damage occurs to the billboard (through no fault of yours)? You need to work those things out ahead of time.
- Don't think you have to go "big" to pull in cash. Local businesses may pay you to display a smaller size poster or digital sign that could still be lucrative.

27. Score hefty referral fees for real estate leads.

Here's a fairly easy way to flow some cash. List your house for sale at a price that would make you happy to move just in the unlikely case that your home would happen to sell. Then collect a referral fee when your real estate agent sells a *different* house to a buyer who originally called about your home or came to an open house at your place.

Prospective buyers generally do not buy the first home they visit or call about in response to an ad or For Sale sign. Most of these prospects become "leads" for the real estate agent, who works with the prospects until selling them a suitable home. It's a bit like dating; you don't usually end up marrying the first person you date or select from an online profile—those folks are just starting points to a more targeted search. A real estate agent can use your home as the starting point to capture leads that he or she then works with until a truly suitable property is found. Upon sale, the real estate agent receives a commission and, in turn, pays you a *referral fee* for the lead.

Here's the Catch

For this one to work in most states, someone in your family needs to get a real estate license so that referral fees can be collected. Otherwise, you could get into legal trouble for practicing real estate without a license! But don't worry; it's not as difficult or time consuming to obtain a license as you might imagine. In most states, all you have to do is take an online course and pass the state test. It will cost you a couple hundred dollars, but the time and money you spend learning the ins and outs of real estate can help you protect and make the most of your single biggest investment—your home.

Once you pass the state test, you'll need to "hang" your license with a licensed brokerage firm. Fortunately, today there are many online brokerage houses that allow you to hang your license for free or for a small sum and then share a small percentage of your earnings with the brokerage.

Incidentally, prepare for the possibility that a buyer could show up and fall madly in love with your home. Buyers in love could pay a premium, and you may find yourself willing to sell. The referral agreement with your real estate agent should include a provision for an actual sale of your home. If you agree to handle showings, for example, you could negotiate a significant referral fee from your agent. Then you can go find an even better *cash cow casa* now that you know what to look for in a potential moneymaker.

Real Estate Referrals pay *what?*

The amount of cash you stand to receive is based on the value of your home. (Actually, the referral is based on the value of the home that sells, which would be similar to the value of your home.)

A homeowner in an upscale Southern California area received two 5-figure referral fees (i.e. each over $10,000) since a real estate agent sold two multi-million dollar homes off that homeowner's house and paid referral fees of 25 percent of the gross commissions. The total amounted to over $20,000 of cold hard cash to the lucky owner of that *cash cow casa*.

As a rule of thumb, multiply the value of your home by 3 percent and then figure 10 percent to 25 percent of that amount as your potential referral fee. So for a typical $300,000 home, you could receive up to a $2,250 referral fee every time an agent sells another house to a buyer who first called about your house or came to your open house.

Top Do's & Don'ts of Real Estate Referrals

- <u>Do</u> select a real estate agent who you can trust to tell you when a sale has resulted from a lead off of your home. First, you should feel confident that the agent would tell you the truth (if they know it). Second, check that the agent has appropriate systems in place to track where a lead came from so they know if your referral resulted in a sale. Selecting your sister or best friend won't work for you if they don't track their leads.
- <u>Do</u> sign a written referral agreement with your agent specifying the percentage you will receive as a referral fee. People, even relatives and best friends, can get amnesia when it comes to the numbers.
- <u>Do</u> base the referral fee on the *gross* rather than *net* commission. Many real estate agents have to split nearly half of the commission with their broker, which would leave you with half as much if your fee were based on the agent's *net*.

- <u>Don't</u> settle for less than a 10 percent referral fee or higher if you'll cooperate with open houses or showing your own house to prospective buyers.
- <u>Don't</u> shortchange yourself if your home would be worth a higher referral fee to an agent. A newer agent, for example, may be willing to pay you more for the opportunity to have a listing that would generate leads especially if you would allow the agent to place a sign on your property and hold open houses. Does your home have "curb appeal" that would cause prospective buyers to call about it? Is it located in a well-traveled location? Is the interior or backyard photogenic? If so, you might be able to negotiate up to a 25 percent referral fee or higher.
- <u>Don't</u> underestimate the power of great pictures. Make sure your agent takes top quality photos of your home and posts them in a multiple listing service that automatically populates to the dozens of real estate websites most prospective buyers use today to search for homes. These sites include *Realtor.com, Zillow.com, Trulia.com* and many others. Remember the main goal is to generate leads for the agent.

Chapter Seven. Special Loans and Grants

In the not so distant past, the popular way to have your house pay you was to borrow more money against its ever-rising value. Refinances, second mortgages, and lines of credit may have created the illusion of a cash cow, but here's the sad truth revealed by the burst of the housing bubble: Increasing your debt does not boost your earnings or create true wealth.

For many homeowners today, borrowing more money is simply not an option when there is little if any equity in the home or when the homeowner has income and credit issues. However, *provided* you fall into a select group of people or own a select type of property, borrowing more money against your home might not only be feasible but also might make perfect sense! The reason is that the government offers several special loan programs that include extremely favorable terms for these lucky homeowners.

Skip to the next chapter if you don't need a loan modification and live in an urban area, unless you are 62 years old or older. These special-case loans have many restrictions based on either the borrower, the location of the property, or both.

28. Let a "reverse mortgage" make YOU payments.

Unlike a standard mortgage that requires you to make monthly payments _to your lender,_ a reverse mortgage allows you to receive either a lump sum or periodic payments _from the lender_. In other words, the lender pays you—hence the term "reverse" mortgage.

The advantages of a reverse mortgage are many. Any lump-sum cash that you get from a reverse mortgage is tax-free and you retain ownership of your home. According to the AARP, the number one reason people take out a reverse mortgage is to pay off a regular mortgage and get rid of monthly loan payments.

Qualifying for a Reverse Mortgage

In order to qualify for this federal government-backed loan program, you have to be a senior homeowner 62 years old or older. You don't have to give up title to your property or sell in order to turn a portion of your home equity into cash. As long as you live in the home, you never have to make loan payments even if the value of your home declines. And if the value increases, you or your heirs receive the benefits of price appreciation.

You'll have to consult with a loan counselor before deciding if a reverse mortgage would work for you. You don't have to qualify for a reverse mortgage based on income and credit as you would for a regular mortgage. However, there are some requirements:

- You must be 62 years of age or older.
- The home must be your principal residence with sufficient equity.
- Participation in a loan counseling session is a must.
- You can't be delinquent on any federal debt.
- Your home must be a single-family home, a condo, an FHA-approved manufactured home, or a 2-4-unit home with you occupying one of the units.
- Also property taxes and insurance payments need to be paid current.

Reverse Mortgages pay *what?*

The amount of cash you can obtain depends on several factors including your age. As an example, an 89-year old senior living in a paid-off home worth approximately $100,000 was able to get a reverse mortgage up to about $65,000. He could take that as a lump sum, as monthly payments for life or for a fixed period of time, or as a combination of payments and upfront cash.

Top Do's & Don'ts of Reverse Mortgages

- Do factor in the rather hefty fees of obtaining this type of mortgage. It's not free, which is why it may not make sense if you're in your young to mid 60's. The numbers work better for homeowners who are 70 and over.
- Do consider this opportunity to enjoy your golden years while staying in your home. It's the closest thing to "having your cake and eating it too."
- Do seek professional advice in deciding how to best structure the reverse mortgage for your situation. A financial expert will help you decide the option that would work best for you: Monthly payments, a lump sum, or a combination of the two.

- Don't assume your home must be paid off in order to obtain a reverse mortgage. Your current mortgage only has to be low enough that it could be paid off by the new reverse mortgage.
- Don't worry if you have credit issues. Although any federal loan that you may already have needs to be current (i.e. not past due), a reverse mortgage is not based on your creditworthiness, as are standard

mortgages, so you could get a reverse mortgage even if you have poor credit.

- <u>Don't</u> be concerned that the reverse mortgage could end up being a burden to your heirs or reduce your Social Security payments. The government takes all the risk if the house loses value, and you or your heirs get all the benefit if the house appreciates. And since money from a reverse mortgage is a loan rather than income, a reverse mortgage is not taxed and does not lower your Social Security and Medicare benefits.

29. See if you qualify for a Rural Development loan.

The federal Department of Agriculture (USDA) has a number of loan and grant programs that could be the answer to your prayers if you live outside of an urban or suburban zone and do not have sufficient income or credit to qualify for a conventional loan.

The USDA defines "rural" rather liberally: you don't have to live on a farm. Of course, major urban and highly populated suburban areas adjacent to urban areas do not qualify, but many small towns and lightly populated areas on the outskirts of medium-sized or larger towns often qualify. Per the USDA, these loans are available outside of cities with over 50,000 inhabitants and their adjacent urbanized areas.

You can check to see if your area qualifies at http://eligibility.sc.egov.usda.gov. Under the section on *Property Eligibility*, click the link for *Single Family Housing*, enter your address, and the map will zoom to your location. You'll find out immediately if your home lies in a qualifying area.

Rural Development Mortgages

A Rural Development loan is a great way to go if you and the property fit the guidelines. Monthly loan payments are based on the borrower's income and ability to repay. In other words, the government subsidizes the loan payments. Recipients can borrow up to 100 percent of the home's value and repay over 30 years. Since 1949, more than 2.7 million loans of this type have been made. For more information, visit http://www.rurdev.usda.gov and click on the *Loans* link.

Rural Development Repair and Rehabilitation Loans

In addition to offering primary mortgages, the USDA offers loans to existing homeowners who need cash for repairs and improvements. With this loan program, you can get cash to make home repairs such as a new roof, replacement windows, heating and air conditioning units, and handicap access, just to name a few of the possible types of repairs and improvements allowed.

The program is designed to help low-income homeowners. To obtain this type of loan, you must be unable to get affordable credit elsewhere and also must need to make repairs and improvements in your home to make it safer or more sanitary.

USDA's Intermediary Loan Program (ILP)

For this loan program, your property must be situated in a rural area defined as an area with a population of 25,000 or less. Again, urban and suburban areas do not qualify nor do towns with greater than 25,000 inhabitants.

The USDA provides this lending program to alleviate poverty and increase economic activity and employment in rural communities. Under the ILP program, loans are provided to local organizations (intermediaries) for the establishment of revolving loan funds. These revolving loan funds then are used to assist with financing business and economic development activity to create or retain jobs in the community. For example, you could use the proceeds of this loan to convert your home to a Bed & Breakfast.

USDA Loans pay *what?*

You may borrow up to $250,000 under the USDA rural loan programs. You have to demonstrate your ability to qualify for and repay the loan. Individuals may apply for this loan as long as you are a U.S. citizen or have been legally admitted to the U.S.

Rural Development repair loans are available up to $20,000. The loans give you 20 years to repay at a mere 1 percent interest rate!

Top Do's & Don'ts for USDA Intermediary Loans

- Do confirm that your property is in an area qualified for this type of loan by entering your address after selecting the *Business Programs* link at the USDA property eligibility site at http://eligibility.sc.egov.usda.gov. Then click the ILP link.
- Do check your local zoning laws to make sure that a Bed & Breakfast or other proposed venture is allowed on your property if going for the ILP funding.
- Do work with the intermediary organization to apply for and obtain this loan. The intermediary is the face of the USDA and can support you in getting the funds you need.

- Don't apply unless you have sufficient equity in your property. If you want the full $250,000, then the amount of your current mortgage plus this new loan amount should not exceed the actual value of the property.
- Don't wait until you have every single duck in a row to call the intermediary. Their staff is there to help you put your application together and document your loan request. They can help you with all aspects of applying for the loan.
- Don't ask for too little funding. If you need to modify your home to get it ready as a B&B, for example, obtain several bids and base your estimates on the highest one.

You can find more information on the Rural Development home page at http://www.rurdev.usda.gov. From there, click the link for *Loans* or search for the *Service Center Locator* to find the contact to call in your area.

30. Get millions from a government B&I loan.

Another loan program from the USDA offers plenty of cash providing you and your house qualify *and* providing there's a business you could run out of your home. Turning your home into a Bed and Breakfast, for example, would qualify and many local jurisdictions do allow homeowners to operate a B&B in areas zoned for residential uses. Check with your local zoning office.

Like the previous types of special loans, B&I loans are normally available in relatively "rural" areas, which include all areas other than cities or towns of more than 50,000 people and the adjacent urbanized area of such cities or towns.

Get Millions If You Qualify

The USDA's reason for providing B&I loan guarantees is to help employment and boost the economy in outlying communities. This loan program is not for providing marginal or substandard loans so you do have to have appropriate income and credit. These loans are made to individuals (as well as to organizations and business entities) provided that you are a U.S. citizen or permanent resident.

In order to get the loan funds up to millions of dollars, you'll need to propose a use of your home that accomplishes one of the goals of the program. Converting your home to a Bed & Breakfast would qualify. Here is what the USDA is looking for in terms of some goals that the loan would help you achieve:
- Provide employment;
- Improve the economic or environmental climate;

- Promote the conservation, development, and use of water for aquaculture; or
- Reduce reliance on nonrenewable energy resources by encouraging the development and construction of solar energy systems and other renewable energy systems.

B&I Loans pay *what?*

If both you and your property qualify, you could borrow millions of dollars under this program! Perhaps you need far less than a million dollars to repay your current mortgage and get the capital you need to set up and run a business. Rate and terms are consistent with industry norms. For example, if your property is worth a million dollars, you could borrow up to $800,000—i.e. an 80 percent loan to value.

Besides refinancing your current mortgage, you can turn to this program to finance new equipment or machinery or even to obtain working capital to run your business. Repayment of the loan can take up to 30 years for a real estate loan, 15 years for equipment, and 7 years for working capital.

Top Do's & Don'ts of B&I Loans

- Do confirm that your property is in an area qualified for this type of loan by entering your address after selecting the *Business Programs* link at the USDA property eligibility site at http://eligibility.sc.egov.usda.gov.
- Do check your local zoning laws to make sure that your proposed business venture is allowed on your property.
- Do prepare to document your ability to qualify for and repay the loan. The lending guidelines are based on normal lending standards.

- Don't expect the loan to fund quickly. This is a government-backed loan with ample forms and paperwork to complete so the process can be slow.
- Don't rely on the lending institution to know everything about this loan. Read the relevant parts of the USDA site so that you are well informed.
- Don't ask for too little funding. If you need to modify your home, obtain several bids and base your estimates on the highest one. Figure in the cost of equipment and working capital. The lender will help you structure the loan accordingly.

31. Enjoy thousands in government grant funds.

Similar to the USDA loan programs, the Rural Repair and Rehabilitation Grant gives low-income senior homeowners funds for needed repairs and improvements. Unlike the loan program, however, the grant funds never have to be paid back—unless you sell the property within three years of receiving the grant.

With this grant program, you can get cash to pay for repairs and improvements resulting in the removal of health and safety hazards. A grant/loan combination is made if you can repay part of the cost.

This grant program is designed to help low-income homeowners. To obtain a grant, you must be unable to get affordable credit and also must need to make repairs and improvements in your home to make it safer or more sanitary. Also this program is for homeowners who are 62 years old or older.

Government Grants pay *what?*
Grants are made up to $7,500. If you qualify, the grant can be combined with a loan for up to $27,500 in assistance. While the loan portion would have to be repaid, the grant is an outright gift and does not have to be repaid unless the property is sold within 3 years.

Top Do's & Don'ts of Government Grants
- <u>Do</u> spend the grant money on repairs and improvements that take care of health and safety hazards in your home.
- <u>Do</u> fix the biggest safety issues first. Then if you still have money left from the grant, you can make more minor repairs and improvements.
- <u>Do</u> keep all receipts and records of your expenditures so that you can document how the funds were spent.

- <u>Don't</u> spend grant money on anything other than repairs and improvements resulting in the removal of health and safety hazards.
- <u>Don't</u> overlook the fact that grants have to be repaid if the property is sold in less than 3 years.
- <u>Don't</u> skimp on labor costs; be sure to hire licensed contractors who are qualified since all work must meet local codes and standards.

32. Reduce cash outflow with a loan modification.
Most of the strategies in this book feature ways to bring in more cash rather than save money. There are a few exceptions and this is one of them since mortgage payments represent the biggest single

cash outlay for most families. Reducing your mortgage payment means keeping more cash in your pocket.

Banks in recent years have been granting loan modifications to distressed borrowers with a hardship in order to help them avoid foreclosure. These loan modifications typically reduce a borrower's interest rate and/or extend the length of the loan in order to make the payments more affordable.

In order to get a loan modification, you have to be able to document a hardship: loss of a job, a dramatic reduction in income due to business conditions, a health problem or the like. Borrowers at all levels of net worth, from low to high, can qualify for a loan modification.

As everyone knows, real estate values have experienced dramatic reductions not seen since the days of the Great Depression. Housing prices have been climbing in many areas this year but had dropped about 35 percent from their peak nationwide over the course of the downturn.[26] The problem with this large drop in home value is that it has made it difficult for distressed homeowners to qualify for loan modifications.

Qualifying for a Loan Modification

Back in '05 and '06, here's what you needed to qualify for a loan: a pulse and the ability to sign your name on the loan papers. Today, many borrowers wouldn't qualify for the loans they already have. Then if they fall on hard times and miss payments, it's all the more difficult and unlikely that they'll qualify for a loan modification.

When a bank modifies a mortgage nowadays, the borrower's payment must include principal and interest unlike those interest-only loans from yesteryear. In order to make the fully amortized loan payments affordable, something needs to give. Either the loan term must be lengthened, the interest rate reduced, or the loan amount itself reduced in order to get the borrower to qualify for the modification.

Banks have routinely reduced interest rates but since interest rates aren't that high now, a reduction often does not result in a sufficient decrease in the monthly loan payment. Banks also are extending loan terms from 30 years to 40 years to help borrowers qualify. Again, the change to the monthly payment isn't that large. In many cases, the only way to make loan payments truly affordable is for the loan amount to be lowered.

Banks are now using several approaches to reduce loan amounts in order to facilitate approval of loan modifications. One approach is to defer a portion of the principal to the end of the loan, making the deferred principal due as a balloon payment at the end of a 30- or 40-year loan. For example, if the loan amount is $400,000 and the bank defers $100,000, then the borrower only has to qualify to make payments on $300,000. The non-deferred principal balance may match the current market value of the home.

Another practice is for banks to forgive a portion of the principal altogether. Of course, borrowers love this alternative but banks are not so eager to forego principal altogether. A more palatable alternative for the banks is to grant a balance reduction in exchange for a share of future appreciation.

Sometimes the bank and borrower find a way to forge a new agreement that works for both. The borrower qualifies under the modified terms of the loan and the modification is granted on a permanent basis. More frequently than not, however, the numbers just don't work, the modification is denied, and the homeowner must face a short sale, deed in lieu of foreclosure, or foreclosure, resulting in the homeowner losing the home.

Loan Modifications with Equity Sharing

Some banks are now turning to equity sharing as a viable alternative for homes that are underwater (i.e., the loan is larger than the value of the house). Although most banks have been reluctant to reduce the amount of principal on loans that are underwater, new equity sharing programs combined with loan modification are proving acceptable to both banks and homeowners. The bank agrees to reduce the amount that the borrower owes in exchange for a share in any future equity.

Check with your lender, even if you've been turned down for a loan modification, to see if they would entertain the possibility of combining a modification with equity sharing of the future appreciation in your property. It's worth a shot.

Top Do's & Don'ts of Loan Modifications

- Do write a hardship letter in first person that brings a tear to the eye. It should be an emotional appeal for help after explaining that you've done everything you can to solve your financial hardship.
- Do talk to others and research your lender on the Internet to discover the "deals" other homeowners are receiving on their loan modifications. If you discover, for example, that other loans are being modified to a 3 percent interest rate, then you can push harder with your lender even when they tell you they can only reduce your rate to 4 percent.

- <u>Do</u> contact your lender sooner rather than later if you're having a financial hardship. It's best to be frank and get the ball rolling on a loan modification while they're still being done since no one knows if loan mods will continue to be done.

- <u>Don't</u> ask for a loan modification because your house has lost a lot of value and is now "upside down." Banks do not consider the loss of value a legitimate reason for a loan mod. You must demonstrate a hardship such as a significant loss of income, medical problem, job loss etc.
- <u>Don't</u> fail to provide the requested documentation. The mortgage holder will want to see your bank account statements, tax returns and more. They want to make sure that you cannot afford to make payments on the original terms before they grant a modification.
- <u>Don't</u> hesitate to bring up the possibility of deferred principal or a shared equity arrangement especially if the bank informs you that you don't "qualify" for the modification now that your income has been reduced. At this point in time, banks really do want to modify your loan and help you qualify for the modification but they may need some out-of-the-box thinking and suggestions.

Chapter Eight. Cash from Equity and Sales

Up to this point, you've learned about dozens of tried-and-true ways to put your house to work for you, complete with insider information about how much money other homeowners are receiving and the do's and don'ts they've discovered. If you want even more ways to extract cash from your property, here are additional possibilities that might work in your situation. As always, consider each one with an open and creative mind about how it could be adapted to your house and circumstances.

We look forward to hearing about your experiences and especially your success stories with any of these promising alternatives. Please share your story at *CashCowCasa.com*.

33. Reap cash NOW by taking on an equity partner.

It's so yesterday to raise *cash from debt* (by refinancing or taking out additional mortgages) with its annoying principal and interest payments. A better approach is to raise *cash from equity*, which means that you sell an ownership stake in your home and share any net proceeds with the co-owner according to their percentage of ownership. Equity financing is more like what companies do when they raise money by selling shares of stock in the company.

Do You Have Any Equity?
Start by doing the math to see if you actually have any equity in your home. Having *negative* equity doesn't count as having equity unlike that line from a Blues song about having *luck*: "If it wasn't for bad luck, if it wasn't for real bad luck, I wouldn't have no luck at all."[27] It's important to know whether or not there's equity in your home.

A quick way to tell about how much equity you have in your home is to check the current market value of your home and subtract the amount of the mortgage from that value. Be aware that this rough estimate only works if you live in a subdivision with many similar homes. Automated online calculators may be extremely inaccurate for custom-built or unique homes: I've seen the automated estimates miss the true value by 100 percent.

Mindful of the limitations of automated values, check out the "zestimate" of your home's value at *Zillow.com*. It will give you Zillow's estimate of your home's current market value, and it should be within about 5 percent *if your home is very similar to neighboring homes that have sold recently.* (For custom homes, contact a local real estate agent for an expert opinion of the current market value.) Subtract the total amount of loans or other encumbrances on your home from the zestimate to determine the approximate equity in your property.

Should the amount owed exceed the value of your home, then your property is considered to be "upside-down" like nearly 1 in 3[28] homes today that are mortgaged. If your home has little or no equity and is upside-down, you'll either have to convince a relative or other private party to invest with you anyway or give a bigger concession to a company looking for future appreciation.

Professional Equity Sharing Companies

There are companies that will give you a lump-sum payment now in exchange for giving them a portion of your future proceeds when you eventually sell the home. The equity agreement could be for 30 years and does not force you to sell your home any sooner than you otherwise were planning to do.

The process works like this:
- The equity partner will determine your home's current market value based on an independent appraisal by a certified professional appraiser.
- You determine what proportion of your equity you are willing to share, generally from 20 to 50 percent.
- After underwriting, the equity partner will decide the amount of the lump-sum payment you can receive based on the value of your equity, the percentage of equity sharing, the condition of the property, and your financial history. A long-term agreement is then signed between you and the equity partner.
- When you finally sell your home, the equity partner receives a portion of the equity proceeds based on the agreed percentage. If your home increases in value, the equity partner shares in the gain.

Realize that equity sharing is not a loan or mortgage. The equity partner cannot foreclose or call any loan since they are not making you a loan. Equity sharing is based on an agreement to share future equity in your property that would be realized once you sell the property.

One such company claims that their equity agreement, "allows you to convert a portion of your home equity to cash without having to sell your home prematurely or borrow against your home… It enables you to receive cash with no interest and no monthly payments – ever."[29] In order to qualify for equity sharing, this company requires that you have 25 percent equity in your home. This means that the total of your mortgage debt is not greater than 75 percent of your home's current market value. Also they require that you have a "history of financial responsibility."

Another equity share company offers a slightly different approach in that they only partner with homeowners who are 65 to 85 years of age.[30] The homeowner retains all of the property's current equity at the time the agreement is struck while the company essentially pays for the option to realize a significant portion of the *future* increase in equity. For example, the company may pay a cash lump sum based on 8 to 16 percent of the appraised value of the home upfront in exchange for 50 to 100 percent of the future appreciation going forward from the time of agreement. The program makes sense for many seniors who want to tap their current equity immediately without having to sell their home or encumber it with additional loans.

Look for more companies offering equity sharing programs in the future as the proverbial pendulum swings away from debt-based homeownership models to less risky equity-based partnerships.

Do-It-Yourself Equity Sharing Arrangements

Before you turn to a professional equity sharing company, check with any relatives, close friends, or real-estate investors you already know who might be interested in becoming Tenants In Common (TIC) on your property in exchange for a share of the ownership. You might not be comfortable asking Uncle Henry for a loan but it's easier to offer him an opportunity to get in on a money-making investment.

In a typical equity-share arrangement, you and your family remain in the home as the occupying partner while the investor-partner pays a lump sum in exchange for a percentage share of the home's appreciation when you eventually sell it. The investor will be named on the title along with yourself. Check with your tax professional for rules that may apply if the investor wants to enjoy tax benefits during the course of the agreement since that situation could trigger the requirement that you pay a rental fee to the investor in proportion to their percentage of ownership.

34. Generate cash fast from pawn & personal equity.

Before you write off collateral lending institutions—better known as *pawnshops*—as being a little seedy (if not a bit scary), consider the facts according to the producers of the popular TV show *Pawn Stars* on the History channel:

- There are about 12,000 pawnshops in the United States.
- Approximately 70 percent of the items pawned are reclaimed.
- The average loan per pawned item is $75.
- The U.S. owes its very existence to the pawn industry since Queen Isabella of Spain pawned her jewelry to fund the expeditions of Columbus to the New World!

Collateral Lending: Pawnshops

Pawnshops are not just about jewelry. Collateral lending makes sense for those items that you don't need at the moment but want to hang on to long term.

You can hock virtually anything. (Have you heard the one about Mr. Ham who bought a pawnshop and named it, what else, *Ham Hocks*.) (Sorry, couldn't resist.) Besides the obvious items to pawn such as jewelry, electronics, and musical instruments, consider hocking items you don't want to sell: that signed baseball from an old World Series game, souvenirs from your travels etc. *Pawn Stars'* brokers have seen just about everything from a 16th-century samurai sword to a Super Bowl ring and even a 17th-century stay of execution.

Be prepared for a good haggle. Knowledge is power and the more you know about your items, the better your chances of getting a fair loan amount. On TV, it seems as if the pawnbroker gives you information about your item's value and offers a reasonable amount to hock it or buy it outright. In the real world, however, you're more likely to find ultra high interest rates and low-ball offers despite some consumer protections that have been enacted in most states. You have to be well informed and persistent to get a reasonable amount for your goods.

Start by doing a little research on the establishment itself. Check out its reputation online and look for customer feedback and postings. If you bring in your items and don't get fair treatment, shop around. There's surely more than one collateral lender in your area. After going through the pawnshop experience, your negotiation skills should be well honed and ready for anything!

Fast Cash and Found Cash

Payday loans and other "fast" personal loans are a last resort for a cash emergency that readers of this book shouldn't need after implementing some of these *cash cow casa* strategies. However, if you find yourself in an emergency cash crunch situation and need cash really fast, a payday loan or car loan/pawn might be the answer.

A personal loan is a short-term loan generally up to $1,000 (depending on the state you live in) that has minimal qualification requirements. You'll need to be a citizen and have a checking account, phone number, email address, and monthly income of at least $1,000. Typically, no credit check is performed and the money is direct deposited on the same day or following day into your account. Or you can walk into a payday lender and walk out with the cash.

For payday loans, the short-term loan amount is repaid along with the loan fees by automatic withdrawal from your checking account on the due date (i.e. your payday or shortly thereafter). Due to the extremely high annual interest rates charged for payday loans, many states limit how much you can borrow in this way.

Getting a title loan or pawn on your car title can bring in more cash, up to $5,000 or higher. Again there is no credit check, but you'll be asked to bring in your vehicle, the title, a set of keys, your ID, and proof of residence and income. The interest rates are not as high on these loans since the lender holds the equity in your vehicle via the title.

Finally, if you want to leave no stone unturned in your quest for cash, check out those sources that research whether you have unclaimed cash sitting around somewhere and offer to retrieve it for you—for a fee, of course. Don't scoff. Over the years, if you've purchased a few homes, financed and refinanced homes or cars, or had numerous other business transactions, it's quite possible that money was owed but not paid to you. Don't go getting your hopes up that a distant aunt passed away and left you millions, but it's entirely possible that you'll find a few hundred or more sitting idle waiting to be claimed.

35. Pocket extra cash from creative substitutions.

If you would never be caught dead with a fake designer bag or knock off designer suit, then this strategy may not be for you. Knock offs can save you up to 95 percent of the cost of the real thing, but if you're a purist who would never fake it, congratulations and skip to the next strategy.

Swapping out Fixtures and Fittings

Take a good look around your home to see if you could make some creative substitutions to unlock cash while you preserve or even improve the look and functioning of your home.

Many of my real estate clients end up substituting or getting rid of various things after purchasing a new home because the items are not to their taste or are no longer needed. One family sold their expensive high-end HEPA vacuum since their new home came with a built-in vacuum system.

Several years ago, I sold a beautiful estate to a client who happened to hate the pair of Italian hand-blown crystal chandeliers in the dining room and the large spiraling chandelier in the kitchen. I thought they were absolutely gorgeous so she gave them to me! I was ecstatic until the bill came to install those weighty behemoths in my own home. Although the spiral chandelier belonged in a grand hall or ballroom, I put it in my family room where it became quite the conversation piece.

"Wow, that's some chandelier!" remarked an antique-collecting friend who walked into the family room one day.

"Yeah, my client gave it to me since she hated it and I love it," I replied.

"That looks just like a Venini—hand-blown from Italy and probably cost over $10,000 new."

"Cool! What's it worth now?"

"It might sell for a couple thousand."

"WHAT? Hey, I like the fixture but not THAT much."

In a matter of weeks, I found a buyer and ended up selling that Venini for a decent price despite the fact that many of the crystal drops were cracked or had been replaced with non-authentic drops. Then I bought a smaller fixture that looked better in my house for a fraction of the sales price and pocketed the difference.

Faux Art—The Obvious Choice

Purists already should have skipped ahead so if you're reading this, hopefully your sensibilities won't be offended by the following suggestion. We all treasure our art collections, but when you need cash, I say, "Make it a fake."

A low-budget alternative to your expensive painted artwork would be to make a color reproduction (as long as it's no longer protected by copyright). Hang the fake back on the wall and sell the real thing for cold, hard cash. Most people would never notice the difference.

Research has confirmed that most people are unable to distinguish between genuine artwork and high-quality fakes although folks do look at a piece of artwork very differently if they *know* it's a fake.[31] So if you do any substitutions, it's a good idea to keep it to yourself. If you must have the real thing, rent top artwork from your local museum for a reasonable fee.

Copyright laws do not protect an artist's work 75 years after his or her death (unless the rights have passed to the estate) so many masterpieces are free game to copy. For a reasonable sum, you could have an artist at outfits specializing in reproductions recreate a masterpiece in oil on canvas. In fact, the reproduction can be painted on a specially prepared canvas along with special oils and techniques that give it a unique cracked effect for a genuine aged appearance.

For more contemporary artwork, sculptures or other expensive *objet d'art*, check online for knockoff counterparts at a fraction of the price of the real thing. (Check the *cashcowcasa.com* website for resources.)

You can pull off creative substitutions with just about any artistic piece that you own. Just so you know, I've been enamored with Vasarely artwork since I visited the Vasarely Museum in the south of France decades ago. If you came to my home and saw Vasarelys hanging on my wall, you may wonder, "Is that real or is it a reproduction?

The answer: "Only my hairdresser knows for sure."

What Else to Substitute
When you're looking around for substitution candidates, don't overlook the contents of your garage. (By now, the reader must be convinced that I have a fixation on garages, but remember, the majority of Americans with children have garages so crammed with stuff that the family cars won't fit inside. It's a treasure-trove for aspiring *cash cow casa* owners). Your garage probably harbors something that you either no longer need or could substitute out for something less expensive.

One day as I was walking through the garage of a client planning to sell his home, I noticed several cargo covers for vehicles that the seller had long since traded away! Sometimes we get so used to our collection of "Stuff" that we don't even realize that we've outgrown something or simply don't need to hang onto it any longer.

Another client's garage had lots of extra marble tiles that had once matched the home's floors. However, the home had since been remodeled with hardwood floors so there was no need to keep all that marble. The homeowners found a contractor who paid them to take it off their hands.

One last thing: If something on your property is incomplete and you lack the time or money to complete it, you're better off dismantling and selling it off for parts. That's especially true if you think you may end up selling your house. No buyer will get excited about the *potential* of a half-finished project that *would* be great *if only it were finished or working*. Sell it off and pocket the cash. Most buyers won't pay for *potential*.

36. Throw 'demo parties' or home sales events.

"Ding, Dong, Avon calling!" In the past, Tupperware parties and Avon gatherings started the tradition of home selling events, sometimes referred to as "direct sales." Today, the array of goods and services sold through home sales is virtually limitless: bath and beauty products, lingerie, gold and silver, legal services, you name it.

Hosting sales events in your home may take a bit more effort to get going than some of the other strategies in this book but once you get the right systems in place, the process won't take much of your time. One leading website for hosting private parties for direct sales likened the situation to a train: "Everything good involves effort. The beauty …of these systems is that it takes less effort after you put them in place. Just like a train, the effort to get it moving sometimes seems like work. Once you are rolling along though it becomes effortless."[32]

Rely on Systems, Not 'Selling'
Home parties that involve direct sales can be intimidating if you think you'll have to become a salesperson and don't want to do any selling. Actually, your role is primarily to provide the venue, invite your friends and neighbors, and collect your cut of the sales.

One home party sales system called *Create a Cash Flow Show* teaches party hosts the organization, planning and prospecting systems that create consistent income in any home party business. "The momentum in your business will become easy when you put systems into place. This system of creating cash flow will work for you when you put the effort into setting it up."

Many of the direct sales programs out there involve "multi-level marketing." Besides making money directly by hosting sales events, you get others to host events and then take a cut of their profits.

Finding Products and Services to Offer

You'll find an A-to-Z listing of dozens of party product opportunities from Art supplies and Auto accessories to Legal services and Lingerie to Wine and Wrought iron at *CashCowCasa.com*. Some require you to purchase and stock sample products to display at the party. Unless you want to turn this into your job, it's better to find suppliers and sponsors who don't require upfront payment from you and who will direct ship the orders that you generate. Then there's nothing for you to do except arrange the event and sit back and enjoy the fun with your friends and acquaintances.

37. Electrify your finances with solar electricity.

Question: How do you charge a solar electric battery?
Answer: By using your credit card, of course!

Like Having a Tenant without the Hassle

A family in New Jersey earns $6,000 to $7,000 annually from their rooftop solar panels according to a story in *The Wall Street Journal*.[33] After installing solar panels on their roof, the family received energy credits from the government that they then resold for cash. The family installed a solar-panel system that could output nearly 10,000 watts of power thanks to a generous state subsidy (available at the time they installed the solar panels), making the initial installation affordable.

Not all states have a similar program, but here's how it works in New Jersey. The state issues solar certificate credits for the power produced from solar-power systems. Since the state requires electricity suppliers to invest in renewable energy, people with solar energy systems can receive certificates and then sell those certificates to electricity suppliers who need to meet the renewable power standards in the state.

Interestingly, the wife says, "To me, that … investment on the roof is the equivalent of having a rental property, except you don't have a tenant."

Net Metering

Another payment scheme operating in many states is "net metering." This approach pays homeowners for any extra solar electricity they generate. Let's say you have a rooftop solar system that generates 25 percent more energy than you actually use. The electric company would be required to pay you for the 25 percent excess power that you've produced.

In order to qualify for net metering, your solar system must be tied into the power grid, which means that your system feeds power directly into the power grid operated by the utility company. Your meter spins forward as you use electricity from the grid (i.e. you're charged for electric usage) and spins backward when you feed power into the system (i.e. you're credited for the electricity you supply from your solar-electric system). The net amount of power consumed will determine whether you owe money to the power company or they owe you money. Some companies allow you to offset your power usage but won't pay beyond that.

Regardless of the type of incentives offered by your state, check our companion website *CashCowCasa.com* for solar companies that can install a solar-electric system with minimal or no upfront costs to you.

38. Harvest a cash crop or natural bounty.

Harvesting a cash crop or natural bounty from your property, even in the city, might be easier—and more important—than you think. Thomas Jefferson once said, "Those who labour in the earth are the chosen people of God, if ever God had a chosen people…" Did you know that our founding father was an avid hands-on gardener who wrote books on the subject, traded seeds with political figures worldwide, and believed that every American should be self sufficient? According to Andrew Weidman writing recently in *Heirloom Gardener*, Jefferson actually risked an international incident when he smuggled Italian rice seeds into the U.S. (a capital offense) upon his return from an official visit to Europe.

More recently, First Lady Michelle Obama planted a vegetable garden on the White House grounds (as did Eleanor

Roosevelt during the "victory garden" era) and published a gardening book entitled *American Grown*. It wouldn't hurt to take up gardening since according to a Washington think tank, "the world's farmers, ranchers, and fishers will be expected to produce more food in the next 40 years than they have had to in the last 8,000 years combined."[34]

Almost a third of American households intended to plant a vegetable garden according to a survey by the National Gardening Association (*Garden.org*). Yet, the survey found that most of us really don't know what to do or how to do it when it comes to proper gardening techniques. And making money from home gardening presents an even greater challenge.

My own foray into backyard gardening started with many missteps. The first time I ever planted lettuce, I was thrilled when a thick carpet of little lettuce leaves sprang up from the ground. But then the lettuce kept growing *really* tall and tasted bitter so I called to ask a relative with lots of gardening experience, "What should I do about my 2-foot tall lettuce that tastes bitter and has white goo coming out of the stalk when I cut it?"

"Stalk!??" she questioned in a scolding voice. "You let your lettuce go to stalk? The only thing you can do now is throw it out!"

Turns out that lettuce plants need to be thinned if planted too close together, and overwatering is not a good idea either since it makes the lettuce grow too fast. Who knew? Fortunately, there are many online resources now to help newcomers to gardening get up to speed fast. Better yet, there are resources to hook you up with an experienced gardener who would love to help yo.

Matchmaking Service for Gardens & Gardeners
Maybe you have enough room in your backyard for a garden but have no idea how to put one in and coax edible produce from it. Now there's an online matchmaking service for owners of land looking for a gardener and gardeners looking for land to garden. Once you find a gardener, you work out an arrangement where they either pay you with produce or pay to rent the land.

Shared Earth is one such service. Their mission statement explains the impetus behind the company, "SharedEarth.com was born out of our own experience finding a gardener online. As we searched around, we found others who were connecting in the same way. We built SharedEarth.com to facilitate this process and create a national land and gardener matchmaking service."[35]

Another solution to getting started if you have zero gardening experience is to find a farmer who will put in a garden for you. A non-profit company in Michigan facilitates "urban farming" by bringing farmers to urban residents who want a farmer to plant and tend gardens in their backyards. Called *Backyard Harvest*, the company re-landscapes your yard with food production in mind.

In a Nutshell: Lucrative Home Gardening Techniques

It's beyond the scope of this book to provide a detailed explanation of how to garden successfully and how to make money from it. Check the website *CashCowCasa.com* for more information on these topics. So here is the gist of how to garden at home and how to make it pay.

Farmer-philosopher Joel Salatin boils down his common-sense approach to growing into three basic points that apply as much to your home garden as to a huge farming operation. In *You Can Farm* and his more recent books and presentations, Salatin explains how to grow crops in a safe, effective, and productive manner without harming the environment or our own health. Here are his top three recommendations, easy as A-B-C:

A. Rely on perennials rather than annuals. So-called *annual* plants such as carrots must be planted anew every season while a *perennial* plant is one that lives for multiple growing seasons. Raising perennials takes far less water and work on your part once you get them started.

You may already have perennials in your yard. Walk around your house. Do you see any rosemary bushes, mint, or other herbs? Do you have a fruit tree, nut tree, olive tree, maple trees, or grape vines? If you don't have perennials already, you could start with perennial herbs since they're quite easy to grow. Herbs also have the advantage of not needing much water since many were developed in the Mediterranean region where annual rainfall levels are low. Sage, oregano, rosemary, and thyme are great candidates for your home garden.

B. Manage water using old-fashioned practices to hydrate the landscape. Do you remember rain barrels and backyard ponds? Catching rainwater was common in the past but now rain-catching is out of fashion in most areas and severely restricted or downright illegal in others. It's a different story in other countries such as Australia, where according to Salatin, nearly every house—even in urban areas—has several 1,500-gallon cisterns under the gutter downspouts. Nowadays, using rain catchment devices in combination with advances in water systems that utilize polyethylene black plastic pipe, you can affordably and effectively hydrate crops.

C. Boost the organic matter in the soil with natural methods. Chemical fertilizers and excessive tillage have killed much of the organic matter in our soil according to Salatin. The result has been soil that does not retain water well and produces food that contains fewer nutrients. The solution for growing vibrant crops starts with avoiding overuse of chemicals and tillage, then adding back organic material.

There are various ways to increase the organic content of soil for growing better crops. Composting is one popular practice and you'll find plenty of directions for composting online. Or you could increase the organic components of your soil the old-fashioned way with some small farm animals such as backyard chickens. Or visit a friend who has a horse or cow; surely they'd be happy to give you some of the final "throughput." Hey, sometimes you have to be a neighborhood pioneer—like Rosalind Creasy.

When Creasy tore up the front lawn of her suburban home several decades ago to put in a vegetable garden, the neighbors were not amused. As it turned out, however, Creasy installed a sensation-looking garden and captivated the nation with her advise on "Edible Landscaping." According to Creasy, "Where folks were growing lawns, junipers and maybe an ornamental tree or two, they could grow a meaningful amount of food, which would be a much higher and nobler use of their soil." Rosalind Creasy has influenced millions of people to grow food in their own backyards. The question is: can home gardens also make money?

In a Nutshell: Generating Cash from Home Gardening
It's important to select crops that are easy to grow and can be sold in a variety of formats and venues. Although many backyard gardeners start with heirloom vegetables such as tomatoes and peppers, herbs may be more suitable from a *cash cow casa* point of view. Many herbs have medicinal value that translates to far more bang for your buck.

One key to generating cash from home gardening is to grow a diversity of specialty crops that allow multiple income streams. According to Joel Salatin, growers should emphasize plant diversity to allow for seasonal ups and downs.

Then focus on crops that can result in multiple income streams. Sell the crop itself, sell clippings and starter plants from the crop, and market derivatives and products made from the crop. For example, if you grow basil, you can sell bunches of basil, starter basil plants, or jars of pesto made from the basil. Same with rosemary: sell bunches, starter plants, and various teas and preparations that have medicinal or therapeutic benefits.

Adding value is the other key to generating cash from your garden. One guy makes thousands of dollars a year by growing just 200 corn plants by adding value.[36]

"I grow a large stalk corn--almost 12 feet tall," he explains. "This gives me two 5' blow guns selling for $10 each. I keep one ear's seed and sell the seeds off of the others to gardeners for $1 per 100 seeds, or about $6 per ear of corn. I sell the corncob after I make it into a hunting dart for $3. I take all the scraps and roots, grind them, then sell them for $1 per pound as ground cover. I also sell the stalks cut and bundled. (I call it *poor man's firewood*.) I sell all I can grow, because many people use it for barbecues."

The point of this story is that you can generate far more cash when you get creative and add value. By the way, 200 corn plants can be grown in a garden that's about 30 feet by 10 feet.

Cashing In on Your Home's Natural Bounty

If your home has a yard, chances are that there is some type of natural bounty that could be gathered, harvested, and sold. Homes on an acre or more have a greater likelihood of producing natural bounty but don't ignore smaller spaces either. Making the most of your home's natural bounty can be fun and a great experience for the whole family, especially children.

Again, for best results, it may be necessary to "add value" to the natural bounty to make it pay off as I discovered some years ago. A woman knocked on my front door to ask if she might cut down and take several dried stalks from century plants growing on the back hill behind our home. I never thought much about those century plants except to notice that they send up long flower shoots amazingly fast when they bloom. (I looked it up—the stalk grows up to 8 inches per day!) I gave her permission to take as many as she wanted and she scrambled up the steep hill and collected several large stalks.

Curious, I asked the woman what she planned to do with the stalks. She went to her car and brought back a long shiny wood-like tube instrument about five feet long resembling an Australian didgeridoo. She put the top end to her mouth and started blowing the most amazing base tones out of that thing.

"I'm an artist," she explained. "I clean and sand it and bring out its harmonic range. Then I coat it every day for several weeks with a resin to enhance the harmonics and give it strength."

"What do they sell for?" I asked.

"It depends on the quality of the sound. A performance quality didgeridoo can bring $500."

"Wow! And to think I've thrown those stalks into the yard waste."

This is just another example that one woman's trash is another woman's treasure. It's a true story that exemplifies the ultimate example of how a totally overlooked aspect natural bounty could be transformed, with a little skill and elbow grease, into a beautiful work of musical art for which others are willing to pay large sums of cold hard CASH!

39. Turn your mineral rights into cash-flow.

If you're trying to make your house into a *cash cow casa*, it helps to make friends with some real estate brokers. That way, you can call up your real estate friends and see if one of them would order a title report for you. Your home's title report could be a fascinating read if it shows that you still own the underground rights to your property. Even if some of the rights have been sold off, you may discover some gems, literally, that you could sell or lease to others.

Your Property's Title Gives You Rights

The ownership of land includes what's below ground—as well as the house that sits above the ground—unless a previous owner has transferred those underground ownership rights to others already.

The term "mineral rights" can apply to various types of subsurface resources such as oil and gas, metals, or other raw materials. If your title report does not show any transfer of ownership for these rights, then they may be yours to sell or lease.

Mineral rights give you the right to sell or profit from minerals extracted from the ground. Minerals can be sold, developed or leased, depending upon what you decide to do. Generally, you don't actually sell your mineral rights. Typically you get some money right away for giving permission to drill (i.e. a so-called "bonus"), and then you would get a share of the oil and/or gas extracted (i.e. referred to as the "royalties").

Getting Your Fair Share

When you sign a mineral lease, you become the *lessor* and the buyer of the mineral rights is the *lessee*, which is generally an oil or gas exploration company. Since oil wells often pull from 40 acres per well, your property likely will be one of many that earn royalties from the minerals a well produces.

Your royalty is based on the proportion of land that you own compared with the area the well services. If you live on one acre and the well pulls from 40 acres, you would receive $1/40^{th}$ of the income times your royalty share. So if the well produces $10,000 and your royalty is $3/16^{th}$, you would receive $1/40^{th}$ of $10,000 times $3/16$, which amounts to $46.88. That doesn't sound like very much, but realize that you can sell the income stream for a lump sum.

Mike Scott writing for *Mineral Hub* advises that you should find out how much of a potential drilling area is already leased before you sign an agreement.[37] He explains, "If most of the area is already leased, then you may have a better bargaining position because they are likely trying to 'wrap it up' and perhaps will give you a more favorable lease in order to help accomplish this. Also, if they can lease everyone, they might not have to apply for a forced-pooling order (common in many states), which costs money."

According to Scott, royalty shares usually range between 1/8th and 1/4th, with the most common being 3/16th's. In leases where acreage is small, it makes more sense to go for a bigger royalty fraction, rather than a bigger bonus. The reason is that the bonus would be only a few hundred dollars, but a slightly higher royalty could add up substantially over time.

Cashing In Your Royalty or Lease

You may already have a small royalty that you receive from your property's mineral rights. If so, you can find companies through the Internet willing to pay you a cash lump sum to buy your mineral interests. There are also oil and gas marketplaces that provide a platform for buyers and sellers to meet. Even if your mineral income is only $100 per month, you could find a buyer willing to pay a large lump sum cash buyout for the future income stream. Check *cashcowcasa.com* for current online communities that bring together prospective buyers and sellers of mineral rights.

$30M in Unclaimed Royalties

Talk about unclaimed property! Over the last 10 years, a Michigan firm that specializes in locating owners of mineral rights managed to find the rightful heirs and distribute more than $30,000,000 in royalty payments that had been sitting in escrow accounts. Hey, maybe you're one of those missing mineral rights owners who is an heir or beneficiary and just doesn't know it yet! (Check the companion website *cashcowcasa.com* for information on how to look for your unclaimed royalties.)

40. Sell an easement through your property.

As a property owner, you have more rights than you may realize. People cannot use your property or drive through it without your permission. Owning the title to your property gives you the right to grant or sell an easement to someone who wants to have a right of way over your property.

Granting (or selling) an easement does not mean you are selling part of your property. You would still own 100 percent of your property after selling an easement. When you grant an easement to someone, it's like giving them permanent permission to access or drive over your property. A granted easement would be recorded as part of the permanent legal title of your property.

Access is the most likely reason that someone would want to pay you for an easement. Look to your neighboring properties. Is there a vacant lot behind you that's landlocked? Would a neighbor gain valuable vehicle access to their backyard if they could drive over your property? Perhaps an easement over your property would open up possibilities that make nearby properties more valuable.

Who would benefit from buying an easement from you?

I ran across a situation where an easement nearly quadrupled the value of a lot. A woman named Susan owned a home in an upscale gated community that did not allow any horse boarding. As an avid equestrian, Susan wanted to keep her horses nearby so she bought the lot behind her home that did allow horses. Although the lot was adjacent to her home, the access to it was over a dirt road and rickety bridge that could not have been more different than the wide road and fancy gates that led to her home.

Cleverly, Susan opened up a driveway between her home and the lot behind it and granted herself a permanent easement (from her house to the lot). When she later decided to sell the lot, she was able to charge quadruple the price since the equestrian lot now had wonderful access.

An easement should be described clearly and exactly in writing. The location of any physical easement that takes the form of a driveway, for example, should be described in surveyor's terms that can be mapped exactly. Then when the easement is recorded, both the surveyor's written description and plotted map of the easement become part of the legal title. Nothing is left to generalities or verbal agreements.

Valuing an Easement

One of the biggest challenges in selling an easement is determining its value to the buyer. One way to establish the value is to compare values before and after the easement. It's a good idea to consult a real estate professional to give you a "Broker's Price Opinion" (BPO) on the before and after values. Or you could use an online real estate site such as Zillow to search for comparable sales and figure it out for yourself.

Let's say, for example, that you have a vacant lot situated behind your home that has no right of access from the street. If you granted an easement across your property to the vacant lot, it would be worth far more money to the owner since the lot then could either be developed or sold to someone else to develop. The value of the lot might increase dramatically if the easement converted it from a non-accessible piece of raw land to a buildable lot. The lot's owner may be willing to pay a significant portion of that differential to you for granting the easement since it would enable a benefit that can be quantified.

Another way to establish the value is to determine how much it would cost to accomplish the same benefit of the easement in a different way. For example, suppose again that you have a lot behind your home that does have legal access to the street but would require a long driveway to be installed in order to gain that access. Assume further that your property already has a side driveway that happens to connect to their property.

If you were willing to grant an easement, the owner of the lot could use your road instead of having to grade and install a brand new driveway. The cost of the grading plus the "hassle factor" and time required to get a new driveway permitted can be estimated and quantified in dollars and cents. Once you have that estimate, you can negotiate a realistic price for granting the easement.

By the way, be aware that any easement you may grant could be a negative if and when you go to sell your property. The new owners may not want someone driving across their property and discount the property's value accordingly. However, if you need cash now and have someone willing to pay you cash for an easement, why not go for it? Once property values rise back to and beyond their previous highs, the easement may not make much difference to your bottom line if you do ever decide to sell.

Not Giving the Milk for Free
Granting an easement for no compensation makes no sense for you as a homeowner since there's nothing to gain and quite a bit to lose. In one case, owners of a vacation home were approached by a local utility company asking for an easement in order to trench and run electricity to a home being built next door. The easement would have saved the utility a more costly installation.

The vacation homeowners sought advice and realized that the utility company in the process of installation probably would cut down some of their lovely trees. Then the home's title would be effected in that the easement would be recorded, which could be a negative if they ever wanted to sell. Additionally, they would have to endure the noise and hassle factor of the installation not to mention the potential liability if a cut tree fell on their house or the trenching unearthed a problem. It makes no sense for a homeowner to grant an easement for free. So when people and companies ask, "Just say, *No!*"

You'll need to consult an attorney and other professionals to help you set up and sell an easement. It will cost you something to accomplish, but when it's all done you can say, "Easements are *easy* money."

41. If permitted, subdivide and sell off the excess.
Subdivision is potentially one of the most lucrative ways to pull cash from your home if it sits on an ample lot. You could realize a windfall by subdividing your lot and selling off the excess while keeping your home. The catch—there's always a catch—is whether or not your local permitting authorities will allow a subdivision. If allowed, subdividing is not likely to be a quick and easy process. So you'll need to proceed with the other *cash cow casa* strategies in this volume while working on this one in the meantime.

Checking the Feasibility of a Subdivision

Each local area has its own unique process for subdivision, but these steps give you the relevant basics for most areas. First, you'll need to do some homework and check into the feasibility of subdividing in your local area.

- Before you start, check local lot values. Here's where it helps to have friends in the real estate biz. Or you can get a rough idea by visiting *Zillow.com*. Type in your own address and then set the filters to show vacant lots for sale nearby. Realize that you may have to invest a considerable sum to accomplish a subdivision so you want to make sure that the payoff is well worth it.
- Look at a plat map of your property. Again, your real estate broker could supply this or you could find it online. The map will outline your lot and indicate its size. The plat map will also show other lots or parcels of land in your general area. You can check to see if any are smaller than your current lot size. If not, you may not be able to subdivide.
- Check local zoning ordinances. Can your lot be divided and still satisfy the minimum lot requirements in your zone? Check into nearby zones as well to see if those zones would allow a minimum lot size that you would need. For example, if you're starting with a half-acre lot (i.e. 21,750 square feet) and want to sell off half of it (i.e. 10,875 square feet), check whether the local zoning ordinance allows lots of that size. If not, you could apply for re-zoning, which will take time but could be worth it in the long run.
- Check local subdivision ordinances. If zoning does allow the size of your proposed subdivided lots, the next step is to check subdivision ordinances. Subdivision laws vary widely from state to state and in recent years have become drastically restrictive in certain areas.

Don't think that because your neighbors subdivided their property 10 or 20 years ago that you'll have no problem doing the same. I know someone who put off subdividing his 10 acres when an adjacent landowner subdivided a similar 10 acres into 4 parcels that he subsequently sold off for development. Later, the ordinances became far more restrictive and the other 10-acre parcel could not be subdivided at all.

In my local area, subdivision ordinances and zoning laws are hyper-restrictive since Malibu borders the Pacific Ocean. As far as five miles inland from the ocean, an oversight regulating body known as the California Coastal Commission rides roughshod over homeowners who want to modify their property. The exceedingly restrictive policies of this appointed body have helped give rise to a popular new breed of consultant known as the "expediter."

The Process of Getting a Subdivision Permitted

Homeowners who hope to get a permit to subdivide are well advised to hire an expediter, who typically has a background in urban planning, law, building or development. Expediters don't come cheap but they're worth their fee since they stay abreast of the complex ordinances and know how to "horse trade" with the governing bodies to get the homeowners what they want. If a top expediter can't help you subdivide your property, you might as well give up on the idea.

- Have a surveyor draw up your proposed plan. If it looks like you might be able to subdivide, you'll need to hire a land surveyor to create the legal description and plot it on a map.
- Conduct any required engineering studies. Your local permitting authorities may want to see geology and engineering studies to determine the impact of your subdivision plan. They may require a drainage plan, for example.
- Submit your application for the subdivision. Your proposed plan will go to the county or city office that issues such permits. It's likely that they will require revisions to your plan (or deny it altogether). If you're using an expediter, he or she will help you through the process.
- Comply with requested revisions and resubmit. You could be stuck at this step for several iterations. You may wonder if the planning department is just trying to wear you down! Again, it helps to use an expediter. If you can't find an expediter in your area, consult with a local attorney specializing in zoning and land use planning.

It's also a good idea to contact a CPA or tax specialist since there are tax implications of subdividing and selling off a portion of your lot.

It's best to get started right away on the process if you believe that it's at all plausible to subdivide and sell off a portion of your lot. Realize that it could be a multi-year process. I know of several situations where the house straddled two legal parcels. One of the homeowners decided it was worth it to seek a lot-line adjustment so that his house sat on one legal parcel and the rest of the land formed a separate legal lot that could be sold. It took years to get the plan permitted, but eventually, the separate lot was formed and sold for a hefty sum.

Chapter Nine. Sharing and Caring

The rise of Internet communities is empowering individuals in ways never imagined just a few years ago. Innovative startup companies around the world are leveraging the Internet by creating online communities that bring people together and change how we interact with others whether they're located across town or across the globe. It has given rise to a new approach to consumption dubbed "collaborative consumption" based on sharing rather than on individual ownership.

Several of the remaining strategies in this book rely on Internet-based collaborative consumption communities that have emerged as marketplaces to hook people up toward a common purpose or interest.

42. Share your car and make $600 a month or more.

Car sharing makes sense and could bring you over $7,000 a year if your car sits unused for hours at a time.[38] Do you commute to work and then leave the car parked all day? You could offer to share it with someone who needs it for a few hours during the day. Going on a vacation and leaving your car home in the garage? You could rent it out while you're away and potentially cover a significant portion of your vacation. Or perhaps you don't need your car on the weekend, or conversely, during the week.

<u>Simple and Environmentally Sensible</u>
Jumping into the new world of car sharing can bring you cash while helping the environment as well. Car sharing is touted as environmentally responsible according to one of the top car sharing companies Relay Rides that states, "Renting out one car through Relay Rides can take an estimated 14 cars off the road, resulting in cleaner air and clearer streets for you and new mobility for your neighbors."[39] Car sharing is the new cool thing to do.

Online car sharing companies let you set the rental price for your car and control its calendar of availability. You can rent your car by the hour, day or week. The car sharing company Relay Rides pays you 60 percent of what the renter pays them to rent the car.

The process is fairly simple. You list your car and upload pictures. There's no fee to register or to list your vehicle for sharing. Then you review the circumstances of each potential rental and decide whether or not to rent out your car.

But is it safe?
Car sharing internet communities allow you to review a prospective renter's profile that includes personal information about the renter, information about the number of trips he or she has taken through the service, and any reviews posted by other community members who've rented to the person.

In the case of Relay Rides, the company screens potential renters to ensure a positive experience. They don't allow renters with a bad driving record or an unconfirmed identity to rent your car. You'll meet the renter face-to-face to check their identity and hand them the keys. Or if your car is enabled with suitable technology, the keys can be left inside and the car unlocked remotely for the renter by the company.

The community aspect of car sharing gives you added protection especially over time as more and more feedback accumulates. By leaving a review after each rental, the reputations of both car owners and car renters come into sharper focus. Over time, feedback leads to a more reliable and trustworthy community that results in a more satisfactory experience for all involved.

As for your car, Relay Rides cover your car with a $1,000,000 liability policy during every rental. You're covered in the event of any damages or theft with no out-of-pocket expenses on your part.

43. Monetize personal items via sharing, not selling.

In the spirit of "having your cake and eating it too," there are now a number of companies on the Internet that can put you in touch with people looking to rent your stuff: tools, gadgets, musical equipment, camping gear and just about anything else you own and are willing to rent to others. Signing up with a rental matchmaker generally won't cost you anything; they build their costs into the fee you pay when someone rents your items.

A Collaborative Consumption Culture
The tagline of the popular *rentrepreneur* SnapGoods captures the mindset of a growing new cultural movement: "Own Less. Do More."[40] It's not very "green" or economic to have inefficiencies in our system resulting from consumption by individuals who can't possibly utilize the goods efficiently by themselves. Think about how often you use your lawnmower, video camera, camping stove, saxophone, or power saw. If you're like most homeowners, you probably use your stuff a few hours per week or per month at best. The vast majority of the time, most likely, your belongings sit idle.

Here's how the process works. You agree to rent out your items by the day, week, or month and also charge a security fee in case things go wrong. After you upload an item to the online rental marketplace and either select a picture supplied by the system or upload your own photos, people wanting to rent your items can contact you and arrange to pick up the goods. Renters either pay you directly or through the site.

Zilok is an international rental marketplace with a local feel that aims to help users "rent anything" from cars to cameras to cabanas. Both businesses and individuals can enter listings on the site. Zilok claims that they are the #1 online rental marketplace. They provide rental solutions in all sectors of the rental market including party and event rentals, car rentals, vacation rentals, tools and construction rentals, tuxedo rentals, sports equipment, and more.

Keeping Your Things, Money, & YOU Safe

The items you rent out are protected by a security deposit that you charge as well as by a company guarantee. If something goes wrong, the security deposit is intended to cover loss or damages. What's more, in the case of Zilok, the company backs up transactions between verified users with a guarantee that if something goes wrong, the company will step in to repair or replace your goods plus provide you with a temporary replacement until they make things right.

The fact that users register on the site adds to the trust factor. Increasingly, these Internet communities ask participants to register with their Facebook or Twitter accounts. You can check out the person before doing business with him or her. Then as the community grows and matures, more and more feedback is shared about each member of the community so that a reputation or profile emerges that allows you to make more informed decisions about doing business with that member.

44. Commercially certify your kitchen then share it.

Once you get used to sharing your car, sharing your kitchen will be a snap once you get it certified or licensed. Depending on the requirements in your state, you may need commercial-grade equipment that is inspected periodically by the health department.

High Demand + Limited Supply + the Web = Big Opportunity

Setting aside the challenges of getting certified for a moment, realize that licensed kitchen space is in very high demand yet limited supply. Again, the Internet comes to the rescue! Online kitchen rental communities are bringing together people with certified kitchens and people in your area looking to rent kitchen space by the hour or the day.

Restaurants and other commercial kitchen facilities typically have their own agendas and don't want to be bothered with kitchen rentals to startups, caterers, cake bakers and the like. One kitchen matchmaker proclaimed, "We have been quite shocked over the last couple of years of research prior to launching this website, in that there are so many commercial kitchens out there, however their owners don't rent them out!"[41]

That's where you come in. Many people looking for kitchen space would prefer a kitchen in a private residence if they could find it. Several kitchen matchmaking websites have emerged to solve the problem of hooking up people with kitchen space to rent out and people needing to rent kitchen space.

Converting Your Kitchen

If your home already sports a large upgraded gourmet kitchen, it may take less investment than you think to get your kitchen certified. You already have the brick-and-mortar space and may have commercial-grade appliances and equipment as well.

Still you'll need to check with your homeowners association as well as with city, county, and state officials on the applicable laws to see if you can operate a business from you home and what it would take to get your kitchen commercially certified.

The costs of conversion could range from minimal to major depending on the characteristics of your kitchen in relation to the certification requirements. Commercial kitchens have regulated sink size, counter space and floor space. You can find out what's required in your area by contacting the city or county planning department.

Licensing information should be available online at your state's licensing website. The state will be able to provide information on food safety requirements including inspections, insurance requirements, taxes, licensing rules, and applicable laws.

Hooking Up via an Online Kitchen Community

Once you get a certified kitchen set up, you'll need to have it inspected by your state's department of health. Inspections can be painstaking, but if you meet the guidelines you'll have a steady stream of renters thanks to new online communities (check the companion website *cashcowcasa.com* for current contacts). These communities allow you to register your kitchen space online along with available times and pricing. Then people who want to rent kitchen space join the community and look for space that meets their needs. You can also check with your kitchen rental community for help with contracts, pricing, and issues of importance in your local area.

The only drawback: the great aromas coming from your kitchen could stimulate your scale as well as your bank account.

45. Share your home office through "coworking."

Traditional offices are so last century! If you have a nice home office that sits idle during the day or even if you work much of the day in your home office, you could tap into the growing trend of "coworking," where people share office space when they need it.

Coworking may be catching on in response to high annual rental rates in office buildings, $28.10 per square foot nationally, despite high vacancies (17.2 percent nationally).[42] Or, perhaps, coworking is catching on due to the rise in freelancers and one-person businesses who seek the camaraderie of sharing.

One shared office site in Austin, Texas provides a homey environment—pass the coffee—where 22 people pay a fee of $250 monthly for a total of $5,500 per month.[43] On average, people are paying $275 to $375 a month to have access to a coworking, open environment that usually comes with free Wi-Fi as well as free coffee, snacks, and basic office supplies.[44] Extras such as a dedicated desk or a private office with lockable files would incur higher fees.

What's So Good about Coworking

In a survey sponsored by Microsoft, the number one complaint of workers who "telecommute" is the lack of face-to-face interaction.[45] People like to have a sounding board and share ideas with others. Coworking facilities actually are replacing the *home office* for many one-person businesses and becoming the *office home* for these workers who need more interaction with others.

Technology facilitates the hookup between people with office space and people who need it. Websites such as *LiquidSpace.com* and *LooseCubes.com* help bring people together. These matchmakers list commercial coworking facilities that are springing up around the country and worldwide. Many of these facilities allow users to come in and use the facility by the hour or join at various membership levels: general access, dedicated desk, shared private office, and individual private office.

The general access option of the typical coworking facility allows workers WiFi access in a common area so the noise level will be higher than in a private office. People are expected to use headphones for listening to music and videos and noise-cancelling headphones if the ambient noise gets to be too much.

A typical commercial coworking office provides members with electronic keyfobs so they can come and go at whatever times they'd like. The facility provides everything workers need—Wifi, color printers, copiers, scanners—along with perks such as free coffee and snacks, and sometimes even free phone calls.

In order to compete with the commercial coworking facilities, you'll need to price your rates lower than the going commercial rates in your area. If you can provide a dedicated desk and a locking file cabinet, you'll be able to charge more. Check the rates at your local coworking facilities so you know what you'll need to charge to be competitive.

Host a Business Meeting or Retreat

Do you have an ample home office, perhaps two, equipped with WiFi plus plenty of comfortable space both indoors and out? If so, you could rent your place for a company retreat that would allow workers to get out of their office environment and let the creative juices flow.

You can handle the rental much as you would if it were a wedding or film location rental, using an online event matching service to hookup with companies that want to book a venue for their meeting or retreat. (See the companion website *CashCowCasa.com*.) Then charge them a fee to have a site rep or someone on call in case the Internet goes down or the creature comforts need adjustment.

46. Collect fees from pros giving private lessons.

Does your property have a pool, basketball hoop, or large grassy area? You could receive fees from instructors for using your facilities to give swimming lessons, basketball coaching, or other types of sports lessons.

Inside, do you have a piano? Charge a music teacher to give piano lessons. Is your kitchen well equipped? Rent it out to a chef who conducts cooking classes. Do you have a separate office with a computer? Let a tutor hold instructional sessions in your home office.

Perhaps your home has a sports court or tennis court. Check the rental rates charged by private sports facilities and country clubs that often rent their courts on an hourly basis. Public courts historically have been free but now cities are wising up and charging for reserved usage.[46] If your rates are competitive, instructors may choose your site if it offers more advantages such as privacy, flexibility, and amenities such as an adjoining bathroom or rest area.

Payment Arrangements

You'll want a written agreement with the instructor that spells out all of the terms and payment arrangements. Sometimes instructors collect an access fee or facilities fee from students if the instructor is teaching a class or series of classes. Students may pay the fee directly to you but you'll want to make sure that the instructor will pay you if the students fail to do so.

It takes some homework to determine how much to charge. For each sport, contact the national or local organization for that sport. According to the USA Swimming organization, for example, the national average for pool rentals is 15 cents per square foot per hour. Backyard pools average in size between 12' x 24' and 20' x 40'.[47] So you'd be looking at about $40 to $120 per session depending on the size of your pool. In any case, local market conditions as well as what the instructor is willing to pay will determine the amount you can charge.

Once you've struck a good deal, you can enjoy the satisfaction of knowing you've helped improve efficiency in the world by not letting important resources sit idle.

Insurance and Liability Issues

You'll need proper insurance in place before renting to instructors and also make sure they have the proper credentials and carry adequate insurance. As one swim instructor pointed out, "Posting signs *Swim at your own Risk* does not release liability for negligence. The signs might as well say: 'Swim at your own Risk and here is our attorney's phone number so you know where to send the summons'!"[48]

Besides your standard homeowners policy, you'll want to make sure you have adequate liability coverage in case of a problem. Umbrella insurance makes sense since it's not very costly and provides an additional level of liability coverage if needed. Also you can add a special business policy or require that the instructor's business policy name you as a third-party insured. It's a good idea to check with your insurance agent.

47. Charge thousands for big private parties & events.

Another approach to flowing cash is to offer your home as a venue for a big private party or event. Several online matchmaking services bring together owners of a venue (i.e. YOU) and people wanting to book a venue for their party or special event such as an office party or company picnic.

It only takes a few minutes to list your home by entering a short description, uploading some photos of your home, and selecting the types of events you are willing to host such as parties, corporate events and more. Most matchmaking websites let you list for free and then take their service fee as a deduction at the time you are paid. Taking and uploading great pictures and adding the appropriate descriptions are the keys to attracting this type of rental.

Matchmaking Services for Venues

One of the best things about an event matchmaking service is that there is a sense of community. You "get to know" the people or companies you're doing business with since social media helps define their identity. Member profiles and community ratings also help build a member's reputation within the community, which gives the member more credence especially as the community develops and matures.

Matchmaking companies typically provide other safeguards as well. In one case, you're protected by Lloyd's of London to make sure your property is covered in case of any physical damage caused by the rental. Members are automatically covered for up to $1,000,000! In addition, you can require that the renter of your property obtain special liability coverage as well. Check *CashCowCasa.com* for information on matchmaking services.

Preparing and Protecting Your Property

You can make thousands of dollars for a one-day party rental if your property can accommodate a large group. Somewhat similar to a wedding, their 1-day party may be your 3-day event due to furniture and tent rental drop off and pickup so the payment actually covers several days' usage of your property.

Your home does not need to be "wedding bell ready" as it would if you were hosting a wedding, but it should be clean and tidy with all systems working including outdoor lighting if the party will continue after dark.

There should be a contract drawn that also clarifies other details. Who will clean the property after the party and when will they finish? When will the furniture rentals be picked up? Will the caterers use the kitchen and when will they clean up and remove their equipment?

Be sure to clarify the starting and ending time of the party and charge a pro-rated hourly fee for overtime. Specify who will be responsible for the valet service and how parking will be handled. You'll also want the responsible party to get a temporary insurance policy that covers you as a 3rd party insured for $1,000,000 to $2,000,000 in liability coverage.

Collect a security deposit to cover breakage and damage that could occur when you have lots of people milling around. Since the libations flow at most parties, you'll want to put away items that could be knocked off easily. As with any type of rental where you have a crowd of people inside your home, it's wise to lock closet doors and close off unneeded rooms entirely so no one is temped to go through your belongings.

48. Enlist help and then offer animal care services.

Consider caring for cats or dogs on your property if you are passionate about pets, have some extra space, and have the time to set up a small business and enlist help from someone qualified to conduct the business while you're off at work. Many pet owners would rather bring their animals to a caring private home rather than a commercial kennel.

Pet Sitting as a Rewarding Sideline or Career

Today more households have dogs (43 million) than have children (38 million). According to Pet Sitters International, an organization that supports people who provide care for pets, the average annual revenue for its members is $48,635.[49] The majority of pet care visits, about 60 percent, require overnight care while the "typical" pet-care visit lasts only 32 minutes and clients are charged an average price of $17.75 per visit.

To get a better idea of what you should charge in your area to board pets, check with several local kennels to find out the going rate for their boarding and other services. Then price your services below the going rate at kennels to attract customers to your home-based care.

You don't have to limit your pet sitting practice to dogs and cats only. The PSI survey revealed that pet sitters, besides caring for cats and dogs (96%), are also caring for other pets including birds (63%) and caged pets (59.8%). So let them bring on the gerbils, parrots, and assorted cast of pet characters! You just might experience a few extra smiles while going the few extra miles for a pet owner and helping your cash flow situation in the process.

Insurance and Bonding

No one wants to think about what can go wrong but you have to be prepared. What if a pet in your care is injured? What if a dog swallows a ball and requires surgery? Unfortunately, accidents can happen and in today's litigious society, you need to be protected.

According to insurance claim stories posted by Business Insurers of the Carolinas, a dog swallowed a sock while in a pet sitter's care and required surgery. Total paid on the claim was $2,448. In another case, a dog was bitten by another dog while in a sitter's care and required surgery. Total paid on that claim was $5,247. Clearly, it's important to secure specialized pet insurance before you get involved in pet sitting for profit.

Here are a few tips from Pet Sitters International to avoid problems in the first place when you're pet sitting:

- Use caution when caring for more than one pet at a time.
- Check with the owners to learn if a dog is aggressive before letting it play with other dogs in your care. Some dogs don't play well with others.
- If your client's dog is bitten or injured by a neighbor's dog or a stranger's dog while in your care, obtain as much information as possible about the other dog and a statement from any witnesses.

Boarding Horses

If you have proper zoning and appropriate accommodations, you could board horses for others. You may not need to be at home every minute, but it does help to have someone working or staying at home most of the time if you keep animals for others since animals need ample water and food. And occasionally, they find a way to get in trouble so you'll need to keep an eye on them.

Horse boarding takes significant setup and infrastructure to be in place. So this idea may not work for you if your property does not already have proper fencing, watering facilities, shade, and space for horses.

A Note about Subcontracting Daycare for People, Young or Old

Babysitting and daycare for children is always in demand but is a very time-consuming and labor-intensive endeavor. It's not something you can do "on the side" while you hold down a job elsewhere, but you might be able to rent your home to a licensed daycare provider while you're away at work all day.

There also is a growing need for licensed facilities for elder daycare and the need should grow dramatically in the coming years as the Boomer generation reaches full retirement age and beyond. Your paying client would be the licensed professional not the seniors themselves, who would in turn be clients of the daycare provider.

Even if you hire a certified professional to conduct daycare in your home, there are so many requirements that the undertaking may be more than what you can manage while you work outside the home.

49. Receive tax credits & other tax benefits if allowed.

"In this world nothing can be said to be certain, except death and taxes," wrote Benjamin Franklin in 1789 and it's still true today. So while this book for the most part does not address how to *save* money on your house, reducing your tax bite and your mortgage payment, as addressed previously, are the exceptions.

Rehabilitation Tax Credit

The rehabilitation tax credit applies to money that you spend to fix up or rebuild qualifying properties such as historical homes. Rehabilitation includes renovation, restoration, and reconstruction. It does not include enlargement or new construction. Generally, these are the percentages of costs you can take as a tax credit:
- 10 percent for buildings placed in service before 1936
- 20 percent for certified historic structures

If the home is in a disaster area, the credit is increased from 10 to 13 percent for pre-1936 homes and from 20 to 26 percent for certified historic homes.

Property Tax Reduction Programs for Seniors

Essentially every state has some type of property tax reduction program for seniors and disabled citizens. If you fall into either of these classifications, it could pay you handsomely to look into the potential tax savings. Check with your local tax office.

Tax reduction programs vary from state to state. Some states provide cash grants for seniors to use to pay their taxes. Some offer tax credits based on age and income. Other states reassess the value of a senior's property, reduce it substantially, and then collect taxes on the reduced value. Others allow seniors to stay in their homes and defer taxes for life unless the senior moves.

Tax Reduction for Farm Property

If your property can be classified as a "farm," there are various tax reduction programs that might be available in your area. Many jurisdictions offer various tax incentives for land preservation programs. The aim is to preserve agricultural and open space lands from overdevelopment and conversion into urban uses. In other words, the tax incentives are aimed at keeping the farm a farm and not allowing builders to turn it into the next subdivision.

These programs are voluntary for landowners who may decide to enroll their land in the program. If they do, the landowner signs an agreement with the governing body to keep their acreage for agricultural or open space uses for the duration of the agreement such as a 10-year period.

In California, the Williamson Act was created in the 1960's to discourage conversion of agricultural land to housing development. Over half of all farm and ranch land acres in California are enrolled and protected under the preservation program. According to the California State Dept. of Conservation, The Williamson Act is estimated to save agricultural landowners from 20 percent to 75 percent in property tax liability each year.[50] One in three Williamson Act farmers and ranchers said in a survey that without the Act they would no longer be able to afford to keep their land.[51]

Taxes can be such a taxing topic! Time to move on to something far more interesting: you and your home's *moolah moo*.

50. Cash in on your property's unique "Moolah Moo."

Frankly, this is a catchall strategy about helping your home achieve its unique ability to become a *cash cow casa*. As a homeowner, your job is to discover the opportunities that your home offers for which others would be willing to pay. It's also your chance to showcase what you have (or what you know) either in your home, virtually, or both.

What's Your Home's Unique *Moolah Moo*?

Listen closely for your home's "moolah moo"—what your home is telling you (mooing out to you) about how it can make you money based on its location and attributes. Hopefully, the previous 49 strategies have prepared you to hear your home's *moolah moo*. Here are some homeowners who listened to their homes and are cashing in on the message:

- Families in Gainesville Florida, a college town, rent out spare rooms (or their kids' rooms) to sports fans flocking to the campus on big game weekends.
- California homeowners on an acre or two in suitable regions plant vineyards and produce their own wine label, also gaining valuable tax advantages.
- Homeowners with dead trees on their property cut them into firewood and sell cords of wood for about $250 to $600 per cord depending on the type of wood and the market prices of the local area where it's sold. Smaller bundles sell for higher prices on a per-cord basis. Incidentally, check the rules in your area before cutting down trees whether or not they look dead. Some species such as the California Live Oak are protected and must be removed via a special process.
- A homeowner I know rents parking space in his ample yard to a nearby TV location rental venue that needs more parking space. The nearby large home hosts several well-known TV reality shows that you probably have watched. The neighbor with the extra yard space makes a very handsome fee to allow 20 or so cars to come and go from his yard while he keeps his day job.
- Homeowners near public transit stations or sport attractions make money renting parking spaces to commuters and visitors.

The list goes on…. Visit *CashCowCasa.com* to read *Moolah Moo* stories from other homeowners.

Leveraging What You Know into Your Own *Moolah Moo*

Take what you know (your interest or work) or what you have (your hobbies or collections) and monetize by showcasing and sharing.

You are reading an example of this strategy. As a real estate agent who has generated cash from alternative uses of my own home, I found myself answering questions and sending helpful information nearly every day to colleagues and clients who wanted to know how they too could make money from location rentals, online selling, vacation rentals, selling easements, equity sharing, hosting special events and so on. I initially wrote down several helpful websites along with some do's and don'ts to send to others so I didn't have to keep repeating myself. The info was slowly growing into a book.

Then I had an unfortunate experience (as you'll read about in the next chapter) that compelled me to let others know how to extract cash from one's house while avoiding any potential tenant-landlord nightmares. *Voilà!* This book and companion website were born.

You can leverage what you know or what you have by using your home in combination with the Internet. What are your interests? Are you a collector? A historian? An *aficionado*? Today with the help of the worldwide web at your fingertips, you can turn your interest into something interesting to others. You can showcase your interest to others first physically at home, then virtually on the web.

Getting started is a matter of organizing what you have or what you know in a way that defines you as the go-to expert. For that, you'll need a powerful assistant.

YOU as the Expert with a *Powerhouse* Assistant

In my former life as college professor, I was no stranger to accessing the Internet to do basic research. But it wasn't until I had a compelling personal goal that I fully realized just what a *powerhouse* assistant the Internet can be.

Over a decade ago, I had to wait nearly a month to clear up a case of double pneumonia before undergoing a life-saving operation. I needed to distract myself with a very absorbing pastime while waiting. I started writing the story of my life dubbed *A View of the Ocean*. As I began describing various stories and events, I searched online for relevant details and was amazed to find that nearly every story could be improved enormously with info found on the Internet.

As I wrote about my childhood summer camp experiences, I looked up the camp on the web and there it was! Its website even reminded me that the high-pitched droning we heard on overnight campouts under the stars came from a locust-type insect called *cicada*. As someone who has done research the old-fashioned way by roaming the stacks in a dusty library, I can tell you that you won't find a better, cheaper, or faster assistant than you have in the Internet!

Whatever your hobby or passion, you literally can become a virtual expert on the topic by spending a few hours conducting Google searches. Find out what others are doing in your area of interest. See where you fit in. Approach your topic as if you were preparing to take on an apprentice. What are the main things or tips that they should know?

As a person steeped in the knowledge of your field, you know far more than others and sometimes that can interfere with simplifying your message to a non-expert. However, as Albert Einstein said, "If you can't explain it simply, you don't understand it well enough." So look up your topic on *Wikipedia.org* by typing your topic along with the term *wiki* into the search engine and then select the entry found from *Wikipedia.org* in the search results. You'll likely find a simplified explanation of your topic in the first paragraph or two. The straightforward info helps a newcomer get a handle on the topic before delving into the specifics and details of the field.

It's helpful to printout those paragraphs from Wikipedia or use them to inspire your own summary of your topic. Frame the intro so you can include it when you create a physical showcase.

Using Your Home to Showcase

When you attract people's interest in something, first they'll want to see pictures or a brief video about it. Then they'll want to read about it and see more pictures. Eventually, they may want to see it for themselves face-to-face or at least have a virtual visit.

Many homeowners with an expertise to share are showcasing their expertise by creating a class or workshop, a gallery, a home museum, a displayed collection, a site visit, or a fieldtrip. The process of creating a physical showcase at home is limited only by the imagination. Do you have a cottage in your backyard? A spare room? A wide hallway where you can showcase your collection or area of expertise?

Make an appealing display that can be viewed by others. If you have a collection, you'll want to arrange it for the easiest viewing in the smallest area possible without resorting to a cluttered look. The goal is for balance to prevail over chaos. If you've pursued some of the other strategies in this book especially the ones involving the clearing out of clutter, you probably came across stray items that belong in your collection. Pieces of a collection have a way of ending up here and there if not already organized into a showcase.

If you're portraying your expertise at something you do (a singer, sports enthusiast, hunter, quilter, gardener, sculptor etc), then you can intersperse the memorabilia and examples of your creations with photos of you in action. Either way, it works well to make your showcase educational. The showcase is not about showing off, it's about displaying something in a way that will cause another person to learn, be inspired, and ultimately do business with you.

One enterprising homeowner who lives on several acres next to an urban area offers a one-hour Saturday class on "Farm Life" for city kids. Each child pays a fee to attend and learns how to collect eggs from a hen house and milk a goat. It's fun and educational for the kids while the homeowner makes a tidy sum.

Another example comes from collectors of vintage dollhouses who showcase the extensive collection in multiple rooms of their Victorian home that they open to the public several afternoons a week and charge an entry fee. They also have a website with loads of pictures for people who cannot travel to their home to see the dolls and dollhouses in person. The website also allows them to sell their related products.

Using the Internet to Share and Monetize

An entire book could be written on this subject and many have been. Suffice it to say that once you have a photogenic showcase, you can take pictures of it for use on a simple website that becomes your "virtual showcase."

You can take this as far as you wish or have time to do. Once you're online, you can trade with others, sell, and monetize your expertise in variety of other ways. For example, you could let others offer relevant goods and services on your site through Google Ads. You can refer visitors to another site they find valuable and receive a referral fee if they make a purchase there. You can allow visitors to purchase goods and services from you directly through your website. The possibilities are endless.

It won't happen overnight but it's all easier than you may think. And nearly everyone is doing it! Jump aboard the Internet bandwagon as you drive your *cash cow casa* to market! Now, *that's* the subject of another book.

Chapter Ten. First Impulse Is Last Thing to Do

If you're like most homeowners who are experiencing financial stress, the first thing you might consider to boost your cash flow is to rent out your own home while you find a cheaper place to live. This strategy is the very <u>last thing</u> you should consider doing since it's more risky than you might imagine unless you're fortunate enough to live in one of those states with tenant-landlord laws that are NOT stacked against landlords. Even for homeowners in those few states, why relinquish your home without first considering the dozens of alternatives presented in this book? However, if you do decide to go this route then proceed with the upmost caution since this #51, like the infamous Area 51, may be better left alone.

51. Lease your home long term and rent a cheaper place to live.

Perhaps lawmakers originally enacted tenant-favorable laws in reaction to tenant abuses in the past, but today the pendulum has swung to the opposite extreme with landlords suffering abuse at the hands of some clever tenants who "game" the system to delay eviction for many months while sometimes driving landlords into foreclosure. We only hear about "tenant rights" and "landlord responsibilities," never the other way around.

<u>My Personal Story of American-Dream-to-Nightmare</u>
Unfortunately, I'm a landlord who was victimized after many smooth and successful years in the leasing business. As a real estate agent, I've heard some horror stories about leasing gone wrong, but still, nothing prepared me for the nightmare that I personally experienced as a landlady. Ours is a country of laws and protections. Or so I thought. Unfortunately, I learned that dishonest tenants who know how to "game" the system can get away with living in your property rent free for many, many months.

In time, a landlord can get gamers out and win a monetary judgment against them. The problem is that the gamers know how to extend their free stay in the property and then use bankruptcy laws to discharge the monetary damages against them when a landlord finally succeeds in getting the matter in front of a judge and obtains a judgment.

A landlord can lose six months rent or more while racking up tens of thousands in attorney fees. The kicker comes when the landlord gets back a severely damaged property while the gamer walks away scot-free. That's essentially my story.

In my case, Mr. Ultimate Gamer-Hustler (Note that 'Ugh' rhymes with 'thug') presented as a sincere, well-intentioned businessman who turned out to be quite the opposite. Less than halfway through a one-year lease, Mr. Ugh quit paying the rent.

Mr. Ugh proceeded to use every trick in the book to stay in the property for free. Eventually after many delays in getting a court hearing, we got in front of a judge and "won" our case to evict the tenants. Although it's uncommon that a California court awards more than a few hundred dollars for attorney's fees to a landlord in an eviction case, the judge awarded us a huge portion of our attorney's fees related to the eviction along with all of the unpaid rent and other expenses. But we wonder if we'll ever see a penny of it.

Luckily for landlords in my state, there is now "rent default" insurance that reimburses you for up to 6 months of lost rent. The premiums are affordable, costing about 25% of the first month's rent for a year of coverage. This insurance came to my state for the first time a few months ago and is not in all states, but it's worth looking into if you're contemplating a long-term lease.

In order for a landlord to obtain rent default insurance, the tenants' credit must check out and they must have a clean background. While credit checks are standard, running a criminal background check has not been the typical practice when vetting a tenant. It's too bad since a criminal background check would have saved us from Mr. Ugh.

The Silver Lining: Every dark cloud has a silver lining and my negative leasing experience is no exception. I believe that when Life hands you lemons, it's time to whip up some tasty lemonade! My American-Dream-to-Nightmare turned out to be a powerful motivator for me to complete this *Cash Cow Casa* project that had been languishing on the back burner for several long years despite good intentions. My bad experience with long-term leasing compelled me to share what I know about alternative ways that a house can generate cash without risking the tenant-landlord nightmares that sometimes accompany long-term leasing.

Long-term Leases pay *what?*

If my own tale of woe does not deter you from wanting to rent out your home long term, you can start the process by calling a reliable real estate agent and typing your address into the search window at *Zillow.com* to get an idea of your home's lease potential. Zillow's "zestimates" give you a rough idea of the amount your home could lease for, but it takes a knowledgeable local agent to give you a more accurate price opinion.

Realize that computer-generated value estimates are based on quantitative factors such as square footage and number of bedrooms and baths of "comparable" homes in your zip code. If your home is in a development with many similar homes, then the computer estimates may be accurate. However, in many local areas including the ones I serve, computer estimates may differ drastically from the actual value. It's best to contact a knowledgeable real estate professional in your area.

Top Do's & Don'ts of Leasing Out Your Home

- <u>Do</u> check each prospective tenant's credit and history of any unlawful detainers (i.e. evictions). Shockingly, courts today often SEAL eviction records as a way to handle the overload of eviction cases. Read my article entitled "Top 5 Reasons Landlords Should Get Out of the Rental Business (Or Tread with Extreme Caution)" available on the companion website. If you're not deterred, check into the prospect's background including any criminal convictions—even for people you think you know! Interview prospective tenants and ask for at least 3 personal references and check with each.

- <u>Do</u> ask for the previous 12 months of cancelled rent checks and employer contacts. Good references and a recommendation from the previous landlord may not mean much these days, especially if the current landlord wants to get rid of the tenants. It's harder to fake cancelled checks. They'll show you exactly when and if the rent was paid. Pick up the phone and call the current employer; ask about the tenant's *future* job prospects with the company. Then research the company itself to gauge its prospects for continued stability.

- <u>Do</u> collect the maximum allowable security deposit in your state or the equivalent of 2-3 months rent. In my state, a homeowner can collect the equivalent of two-months rent as security if the home is unfurnished and an amount equivalent to three months rent if furnished (in addition to the first month's rent).

- <u>Don't</u> try to lease your home without the help of a professional Realtor. The agent will help screen the tenant, prepare a written lease to protect your interests, and will be knowledgeable about the rules in your state and local area.

- <u>Don't</u> place too much emphasis on a credit report since it gives just one piece of data at one point in time about the prospective tenant. If the credit is poor, consider the reasons why. Prospects with great credit could lose it a few months later if they become unemployed. If income and other factors appear strongly positive, you could ask prospects with poor credit to prepay the rent for three to six months or more (plus the security deposit).
- <u>Don't</u> go without rent default insurance if it's available in your area. These insurance plans may pay up to six months of lost rent due to eviction and up to three months' rent for other adverse situations that could arise. (Check the website *CashCowCasa.com* for details on available insurance plans.) The insurance company will require a criminal background check rather than just the typical credit check and search for previous unlawful detainers. It can help screen that 1-in-1000 gamer who you want to avoid.

Chapter Eleven. Share Your "Moolah Moo"

For many homeowners, their homes are so far *upside down* in today's market that there is simply no hope of getting back to even in the foreseeable future. Even if they jump to the last resort and try to lease their house in the residential market, it may only command half of the rental amount needed to cover the mortgage payments and other monthly expenses of carrying the property.

In that case, foreclosure may seem inevitable. But first…

• Check our website at *CashCowCasa.com* for more resources and details in putting these 51 strategies to work for you. We invite you to share your story of how these strategies have worked for you. Or tell others of additional strategies you've discovered for pulling cash from your house that have worked for you already or that you're trying out currently.

• If all else fails, consider a "Short sale" of your current home and later acquire a property that has a better potential of becoming a *cash cow casa*. A short sale refers to a sale where the loan is larger than the home's sales price—i.e. you sell your home for less than what you owe on the mortgage.

In order to obtain a short sale, the homeowner must be experiencing a hardship and the mortgage holder must approve the sale, agreeing to take less than the current mortgage balance. A local real estate agent knowledgeable about short sales can explain the benefits to you. As an alternative to foreclosure, a short sale generally offers important advantages.

Then who says you can't <u>rent</u> a *cash cow casa* until you're ready to buy your very own home and turn it into a *cash cow casa*.

Happy *moolah mooing* all the way to the bank!

List of 51 Ways

1. Garner thousands per day to host commercials.
2. Get top money for TV programs or feature films.
3. Collect big bucks to have a music video.
4. Book a reality television show for gobs of cash.
5. Get paid handsomely for still photo shoots.
6. Host a wedding for a lucrative cut.
7. Rent out your fully furnished home short-term.
8. Secure cash upfront for vacation rentals.
9. Monetize spare rooms with a Bed & Breakfast.
10. Add to your coffers with a "Virtual B&B."
11. Bring in steady cash-flow from a roommate.
12. Generate income from a makeshift guesthouse.
13. Rent out your garage as a studio or office.
14. Charge well for RV space rentals with hookups.
15. Rent out your garage as storage space.
16. Sell parking by the day, week, or month.
17. Pick up extra bucks from vehicle storage.
18. Earn money from storage container rentals.
19. Cash in store credits after "reverse shopping."
20. Start selling online as an Amazon merchant.
21. Sell virtually anything on eBay.
22. Connect with local buyers through Craigslist.
23. Recycle and "scrap" for cash.
24. Unlock cash fast with a yard or garage sale.
25. Collect lots of easy cash for tower leases.
26. Let advertisers pay you to display their ads.
27. Score hefty referral fees for real estate leads.
28. Let a "reverse mortgage" make YOU payments.
29. See if you qualify for a Rural Development loan.
30. Get millions from a government B&I loan.
31. Enjoy thousands in government grant funds.
32. Reduce cash outflow with a loan modification.
33. Reap cash NOW by taking on an equity partner.
34. Generate cash fast from pawn & personal equity.
35. Pocket extra cash from creative substitutions.
36. Throw 'demo parties' or home sales events.
37. Electrify your finances with solar electricity.
38. Harvest a cash crop or natural bounty.
39. Turn your mineral rights into cash-flow.
40. Sell an easement through your property.
41. If permitted, subdivide and sell off the excess.
42. Share your car and make $600 a month or more.
43. Monetize personal items via sharing, not selling.
44. Commercially certify your kitchen then share it.
45. Share your home office through "coworking."
46. Collect fees from pros giving private lessons.
47. Charge thousands for big private parties & events.
48. Enlist help and then offer animal care services.
49. Receive tax credits & other tax benefits if allowed.
50. Cash in on your property's unique "Moolah Moo."
51. Lease your home long term and rent a cheaper place to live.

Footnotes

1 Stan Humphries, "Despite Home Value Gains, Underwater Homeowners Owe $1.2 Trillion More than Homes' Worth." *Zillow.com*, May 24, 2012. Retrieved from the Internet on Aug 10, 2012 at <http://www.zillow.com/visuals/negative-equity>.

2 Ibid.

3 Jeanne Arnold, Anthony Graesch, Elinor Ochs, & Enzo Ragazzini. *Life at Home in the Twenty-first Century: 32 Families Open their Doors.* Cotsen Institute of Archaeology, 2012.

4 Census figures. Retrieved from the Internet on Sept 14, 2012 at http://www.census.gov/const/C25Ann/sftotalmedavgsqft.pdf.

5 Rose Quint, "The New Home in 2015" *National Association of Home Builders.* The report can be purchased at http://www.nahb.org/product_details.aspx?forSaleID=3082; Summary available as a courtesy of HousingEconomics.com.

6 Richard Verrier, "Los Angeles losing the core of its TV production to other states." *Los Angeles Times*, Aug 15, 2012. Retrieved online Sept 18, 2012 at <http://articles.latimes.com/2012/aug/15/business/la-fi-ct-runaway-tv-20120814>.

7 Vacational Rentals by Owner. Retrieved 9/18/2012 at http://www.vrbo.com/global/advantages.htm.

8 "The Top Seven Reasons Vacation Rentals Tower Over Hotels," *Home Away.* Retrieved 9/18/2012 at <http://www.homeaway.com/info/media-center/presskit/vrs-over-hotels>

9 Ari Levy & Dan Levy, "Homeowners Use Airbnb Room-Renting Site to Pay Mortgage, Dodge Foreclosure." *Bloomberg*, July 18, 2010.

10 10K Vacation Rentals. Retrieved 9/18/2012 at <http://www.10kvacationrentals.com/> .

11 "Understanding the Upside," *HomeAway.* Retrieved 9/18/2012 at http://getstarted.homeaway.com/income.

12 "B&B Tips: Is innkeeping for me?" *BeadandBreakfast.com.* Retrieved from the Internet on 9/19/2012 at <http://www.bedandbreakfast.com/report/summer-07/Tips.htm>

13 "B&B Traveler Trends," Survey of B&B Travelers, *BedandBreakfast.com.* Retrieved from the Internet on 9/19/2012 at http://www.bedandbreakfast.com/about/pressRoom.aspx.

14 Bruce Upbin, "Airbnb Could Have More Rooms Than Hilton by 2012.'' *Forbes.* 6/29/2011.. Available at http://www.forbes.com/sites/bruceupbin/2011/06/29/airbnb-could-have-more-rooms-than-hilton-by-2012.

15 Ari Levy & Dan Levy, "Homeowners Use Airbnb Room-Renting Site to Pay Mortgage, Dodge Foreclosure." *Bloomberg*, July 18, 2010.

16 Ari Levy & Dan Levy, "Homeowners Use Airbnb Room-Renting Site to Pay Mortgage, Dodge Foreclosure." *Bloomberg*, July 18, 2010.

17 "FactSheet," *Self Storage Association.* Retrieved from the Internet on 1/21/2012 at <http://www.selfstorage.org/ssa/Content/NavigationMenu/AboutSSA/FactSheet/default.htm>

18 Jack Feuer, "The Clutter Culture," *UCLA Magazine.* July 2012 p. 41-44.

19 "How to Get a Cell Tower on Your Property," *Cell Tower Attorney.* Retrieved from the Internet 1/29/2010 at <http://www.celltowerattorney.com/how-to-get-a-cell-tower-on-your-property.html>.

20 "How do you get a cell phone tower or cell site on your property?" *Steel in the Air.* Retrieved from the Internet 1/29/2010 at <http://www.steelintheair.com/Get-a-Cell-Tower-on-your-Property.html>

21 "Cell Tower Lease Rates Exposed," *Airwave Management.* Retrieved from the Internet on 9/20/2012 at <http://www.airwavemanagement.com/>.

22 "Cell Tower Lease Rates Are Only As Good As The Terms You Agreed To." *Airwave Management.* Retrieved from the Internet on 9/20/2012 at <http://www.airwavemanagement.com/>.

23 "Facts and Figures," *Outdoor Advertising Association of America.* Retrieved from the Internet on 9/20/2012 at <http://www.oaaa.org/marketingresources/factsandfigures.aspx>.

24 Thomas Gunter, "How To Maximize Your Real Estate Cash Income," *B.Collection.* Dec 5, 2012. Retrieved from the Internet on May 12, 2012 at <http://www.blogs-collection.com/how-to-maximize-your-real-estate-cash-income-95334.html>.

25 Ben Forer, "Get Your Mortgage Paid for by Turning Your House Into a Billboard," *ABC News*, Feb 29, 2012. Retrieved 3/16/12 at <http://abcnews.go.com/blogs/business/2012/02/get-your-mortgage-paid-for-by-turning-your-house-into-a-billboard/>

26 Tim Mullaney, "Home price index shows gains in all 20 cities in May." *USA Today*, Jul 31, 2012. Retrieved from the Internet on Sept 7, 2012 at <http://www.usatoday.com/money/economy/housing/story/2012-07-31/case-shiller-home-price-index-may/56605632/1>.

27 A well-known Blues singer Albert King made this line famous among Blues aficionados.

28 Stan Humphries, "Despite Home Value Gains, Underwater Homeowners Owe $1.2 Trillion More than Homes' Worth." *Zillow.com*, May 24, 2012. Available at <http://www.zillow.com/visuals/negative-equity>.

29 First Rex at www.1rex.com.

30 EquityKey.com. As of Sept 25, 2012 the company had not yet restarted the funding of equity share agreements but plans to fund agreements yet this year.

31 Nadia Khomami, "Our brains respond differently to 'fake' art," The *Telegraph*, Dec 6, 2011. Retrieved online Sept 3, 2012 at <http://www.telegraph.co.uk/culture/art/art-news/8937869/Our-brains-respond-differently-to-fake-art.html>.

32 Deb Bixler, "Create Cash Flow in Home Party Business." *CreateaCashflowShow.com.* Retrieved from the Internet on Sept 20, 2012 at http://www.createacashflowshow.com/cash-flow/generate-cash-after-the-show.htm.

33 Diana Ransom, "Putting Your House to Work." *The Wall Street Journal*, U.S. Edition Home, Dec 2, 2008.

34 Dan Glickman, "Expanding Food Production in a Carbon Constrained Future." *The Aspen Leaf*, Aug 28, 2012.

35 Mission Statement, *SharedEarth.com.* Retrieved from the Internet on Sept 13, 2012 at <http://www.sharedearth.com/mission>

36 Bill Donze, "He gets $30 for a corn stalk!" Sidebar to Ken Scharabok, "Can your garden provide homestead income?" *Countryside & Small Stock Journal*. Retrieved from the Internet on Sept 19, 2012 at <http://www.countrysidemag.com/issues/86/86-2/Ken_Scharabok.html>.

37 Mick Scott, "Oil and Gas Leasing Tips." *Mineral Hub*, Sept 19, 2010. Retrieved online on Sept 6, 2012 at <http://www.mineralhub.com/2010/09/oil-and-gas-leasing-tips-part-one/>

38 Claim made by the Relay Rides website relayrides.com.

39 Stats from the Relay Rides website *relayrides.com*.

40 Slogan from SnapGoods at *www.snapgoods.com*.

41 Rent a Kitchen FAQ. Retrieved online 9/12/2012 at <http://www.rentakitchen.com.au/frequently-asked-questions>.

42 Elaine Misonzhnik, "Class-A Office Leasing Picks Up, Mostly in Gateway Markets." *National Real Estate Investor*, June 13, 2012. Retrieved from the Internet on 8/24/12 at <http://nreionline.com/property/office/class-a-office-leasing-picks-up-mostly-in-gateway-markets/>.

43 Jon Swartz, "New trend: 'Co-working,' where people share office space." *USA Today*, Technology, Mar 18, 2010. Retrieved online on Sept 5, 2012 at http://usatoday30.usatoday.com/tech/news/2010-03-18-coworking18_ST_N.htm.

44 Eileen Zimmerman, "Putting a Shared Office to the Test." *The New York Times*, July 30, 2011. Retrieved from the Internet on July 18, 2012 at http://www.nytimes.com/2011/07/31/jobs/31career.html?_r=0.

45 Jon Swartz, "New trend: 'Co-working,' where people share office space." *USA Today*, Technology, Mar 18, 2010. Retrieved online on Sept 5, 2012 at http://usatoday30.usatoday.com/tech/news/2010-03-18-coworking18_ST_N.htm.

45 Eileen Zimmerman, "Putting a Shared Office to the Test." *The New York Times*, July 30, 2011. Retrieved from the Internet on July 18, 2012 at <http://www.nytimes.com/2011/07/31/jobs/31career.html?_r=0>.

46 The city of Louiseville Kentucky, for example, charges for rental of their sports facilities if you want to reserve a particular time. Retrieved from the Internet on July 14, 2012 at <http://www.louisvilleky.gov/MetroParks/rentals>.

47 Swimming Pool, *Wikipedia*. Retrieved online on Sept 6, 2012 as <http://en.wikipedia.org/wiki/Swimming_pool>

48 Sue Nelson, "Can I Rent Your Pool?" *USA Swimming*. Retrieved Sept 6, 2012 at <http://www.usaswimming.org/ViewMiscArticle.aspx?TabId=1755&Alias=rainbow&Lang=en&mid=7714&ItemId=3541>

49 "Professional Pet Sitters Benefit from Increased Demand." *Pet Sitters International*. Retrieved on 9/10/12 at <http://www.petsit.com/2011-soi-results>

50 State of California, Dept. of Conservation. Retrieved from the Internet on Sept 8, 2012 at <http://www.consrv.ca.gov/dlrp/lca/basic_contract_provisions/Pages/index.aspx>

51 *Land in the Balance*. University of California: December 1989. Retrieved from the Internet on Sept 8, 2012 at http://www.consrv.ca.gov/dlrp/lca/basic_contract_provisions/Pages/index.aspx